THE HOME EQUITY LENDING INDUSTRY: REFINANCING MORTGAGES FOR BORROWERS WITH IMPAIRED CREDIT

JOHN C. WEICHER

The Home Equity Lending Industry:
Refinancing Mortgages for Borrowers with Impaired Credit

John C. Weicher

Hudson Institute

Hudson Institute

ISBN 1-55813-065-9
Copyright © 1997 Hudson Institute, Inc.
Second Printing, November 1997

Printed in the United States of America

This book may be ordered from :
Hudson Institute
Herman Kahn Center
P.O. Box 26-919
Indianapolis, Indiana 46226
(317) 545-1000
or 1-800-HUDSON-0

TABLE OF CONTENTS

LIST OF TABLES

LIST OF FIGURES

ACKNOWLEDGMENTS

This study of the home equity lending industry was undertaken at the request and with the support of the Home Equity Lenders Leadership Organization (HELLO). It should therefore be stated clearly that the analysis, conclusions, and opinions in the study are entirely my own, and not necessarily those of the members of HELLO or its directors. The role of the HELLO members has been to provide information concerning the business activities of their respective firms. This has not been a small task. The fact that there has been no previous study of the home equity lending industry from a public policy perspective means that individual lenders have not organized their management information systems to provide the kind of data I have needed.

For their assistance, without which the study could not have been completed, I am grateful first to the members of the Board of Directors of HELLO: Gary K. Judis, President and CEO, Aames Financial Corporation, and Chairman of HELLO; J. Terrell Brown, CEO and Chairman of the Board, United Companies Financial Corporation, Co-Chairman of HELLO; Robert Grosser, President, Cityscape Corporation; Sidney A. Miller, Chairman, Delta Funding Corporation; and

James E. Moore, President and CEO, ContiFinancial Corporation. Their support for the study was essential; it ensured that I received the necessary information. I am also grateful to many individuals at the various member firms who directly provided the information to me. Often they have gone well beyond their standard reporting to provide special tabulations, at a significant cost in time and resources. Besides providing information, they have patiently answered my questions and requests for clarification. I know that many more individuals helped, besides those with whom I spoke, and I want to express my thanks to all of them.

Other individuals have provided substantial and important assistance. Dan Feshbach, President and CEO, Mortgage Information Corporation, generously made available special tabulations from MIC's database of both prime and subprime mortgages, providing a valuable component of the study. Grant Harvey, Regional Account Manager for MIC, compiled the data and answered my questions. Warren Lasko, executive vice president of the Mortgage Bankers Association of America, was also generous in giving me access to information from MBA's surveys of its membership; these data enabled me to create a context for the business activities of home equity lenders. Douglas Duncan, Senior Economist at MBA, provided the detailed information. Jeanne Hogarth, at the Board of Governors of the Federal Reserve System, made available unpublished tabulations on home equity lending from the Board's new Survey of Consumers. I am grateful to Salomon Brothers for permission to reproduce figure 4.1.

My research assistant, Adam Goldin, was consistently helpful over the duration of the study, most particularly in preparing the figures. S.T. Karnick edited the manuscript and prepared the study for publication.

Executive Summary

This monograph is the first systematic study of the home equity lending industry from a public policy perspective. As defined in this study, home equity lending is the process of refinancing mortgages for homeowners whose credit ratings do not meet the normal underwriting standards of prime lenders. There are two dimensions to this definition: the nature of the loan, and the credit standing of the borrower. Home equity loans are first liens on homes already owned by their occupants. They are not purchase money mortgages, second mortgages, or home equity lines of credit, although the term "home equity lending" has sometimes been applied to the latter two instruments. The borrowers are individuals with some history of credit problems.

Home equity lending is a rapidly growing and changing sector of the home mortgage market but is not very well known or understood outside the industry itself. It is so new that there are no standard measures of its size. It appears to account for 5 to 10 percent of total mortgage originations in the U.S. Ten years ago, it was perhaps one-half to one-tenth its current size. Nor is there a standard descriptive terminology: the industry is variously called *subprime lending, B&C lending,* and *the nonconforming market,* as well as home equity lending. Similarly, the firms active in subprime lending are not readily identified in the public mind. They are best described as home equity lenders today, but in the past they have more often been termed finance companies.

Information for the study came from several sources: data provided by individual member firms of the Home Equity Lenders Leadership Organization (HELLO); aggregate information on subprime lending from the Mortgage Information Corporation (MIC), covering a large sample of prime and subprime lenders; the Mortgage Bankers Association of America (MBA); published reports of Wall Street analysts; securities prospectuses of HELLO member firms; and the trade press and general media. The data cover different firms, subjects, and time periods, and therefore are not always fully consistent. Nonetheless, they all present the same basic picture of home equity lending.

The Process of Home Equity Lending

Credit standards in mortgage markets are effectively established by the two large government-sponsored enterprises (GSEs), the Federal National Mortgage Association (FNMA or Fannie Mae) and the Federal Home Loan Mortgage Corporation (FHLMC or Freddie Mac). These firms buy or securitize loans that meet their underwriting standards, and these debts are known as *prime* or *agency* loans. Home equity lenders specialize in *subprime* loans, those to borrowers with impaired credit. Such borrowers are typically seeking to refinance a current mortgage at a lower rate or to take cash out of home equity for purposes important to them.

The loans may be initiated in several ways. The most common method is through a correspondent, a lender with a warehouse line of credit provided by a bank or other financial institution, which then sells the loan to another lender. Alternatively, loans are purchased wholesale from mortgage brokers. Approximately one-sixth are originated in retail offices which establish direct contact with potential borrowers.

The loans are then usually packaged as securities and sold to investors through Wall Street firms, in the same manner as traditional mortgage-backed securities issued by the GSEs or other prime lenders.

In sharp contrast to the prime mortgage market, there are no generally accepted underwriting guidelines for subprime home equity lenders. Individual firms set their own guidelines. They typically take the same factors into consideration but set different criteria to qualify for a given credit grade. Hence, one firm's B loans may look like another's C loans. Underwriting appears to be an art rather than a science. For this reason, subprime loans cannot be treated as a standard commodity, again in contrast to loans in the prime market.

The industry is not dominated by one or a few firms. Most firms concentrate their operations within a particular geographical region, although most also have at least a few loans from nearly every state.

Many are expanding their geographic range of operations.

The Growth of Home Equity Lending

Home equity lending today probably exceeds $100 billion annually. It has grown rapidly for several reasons. The failure of many savings and loan associations (S&Ls) in the late 1980s resulted in legislation that strengthened the market position of the GSEs, along with new regulations curtailing the ability of S&Ls to take risks. Also, the unprecedented peacetime inflation of 1965-1980 drove home prices up in both nominal and real terms, and they have remained generally high even though the inflation rate has been much lower since 1982. Many homeowners have therefore enjoyed increases in their home equity, but because their credit rating does not meet GSE standards, they have not been able to refinance in the prime mortgage market. As a result, home equity lending to subprime borrowers has increased at an extraordinary rate during the last five to ten years.

Demographic and Economic Characteristics of Borrowers

In most respects, subprime home equity borrowers are similar to other homeowners. Their median income is approximately $34,000, slightly below the $37,000 median for all homeowners and almost exactly the same as the $34,000 median for all U.S. households. The difference between home equity borrowers and all homeowners arises because there have been few high-income borrowers in the subprime home equity market. Otherwise, the income distributions are similar. Home equity borrowers are not concentrated among low-income homeowners.

Home equity borrowers tend to be slightly younger than all homeowners, even though it takes time to build up enough equity to borrow against. This pattern occurs because elderly homeowners are substantially underrepresented among home equity borrowers. The typical home equity borrower is forty-eight years old, compared to fifty-one for all homeowners. Single men are twice as common among subprime home equity borrowers as among all homeowners. Single women are somewhat underrepresented.

These data suggest that subprime home equity borrowers are basically the same sort of people as other homeowners and are able to make informed judgments about what is in their own best interests. They are not particularly concentrated among the elderly or families headed by a single woman, groups sometimes thought to be most vulnerable to predatory practices in housing-related transactions. Direct data on the education of subprime home equity borrowers are not available, but education tends to be correlated with income, and there is no evidence that subprime borrowers are concentrated among poor households. Thus there is no particular reason to think that subprime home equity borrowers are less well educated than all homeowners.

Mortgage Rates and Terms

Interest rates in the subprime home equity loan market are higher than the rates on prime loans, because subprime lenders face higher servicing costs and assume more risk. Data from the Mortgage Information Corporation indicate that subprime loans carry an annual interest rate of approximately 11 percent, compared to 8 percent for prime mortgages. For the same reason, interest rates vary among different credit grades within the subprime market: lenders charge higher rates on loans expected to be riskier. These rates tend to rise or fall together in response to conditions in the financial markets. Wall Street analysts estimate that the least risky loans run approximately 200 basis points above prime mortgages; the most risky, approximately 600 basis points. These spreads are not immutable; they vary from time to time and are likely to do so in the future.

HELLO member data also show that interest rates are higher on loans to borrowers with lower credit ratings. The spreads differ somewhat from the Wall Street estimate: HELLO members report a range of 500 basis points between their least risky and most risky loan, wider than the 400 basis point estimate of Wall Street analysis. HELLO data show that LTVs and loan amounts are both higher on higher-quality loans. The overall pattern is clear and not surprising: rates are higher, and terms less generous, on riskier loans.

Subprime rates typically lie between the rates on prime mortgages and those on credit card debt. Because even the highest interest rates on subprime home equity loans are lower than the interest rates charged on consumer credit cards, a homeowner who faces a high debt burden or unexpected costs may well find it in his or her best economic interests to refinance a mortgage rather than to borrow directly or indirectly against a credit card.

Subprime mortgages have an average loan-to-value ratio (LTV) of 72 percent. The typical loan amount is approximately $60,000 to $65,000. The LTV is slightly lower than the median LTV for prime conventional mortgages—75 percent—and much lower than the median, 97 percent, for government-guaranteed loans (FHA and VA). The loan amount is well below the typical prime conventional loan of $85,000, and close to the typical government-guaranteed loan amount of $60,000. Subprime loans also tend to have shorter maturities, most commonly fifteen years, with an average of approximately twenty years; conventional prime and government-guaranteed mortgages typically have thirty-year terms.

Origination and Servicing Costs

Origination costs appear to be substantially higher for subprime mortgages, in the range of 4 to 8 percent, compared with an average of 2 percent for prime mortgages. Servicing costs are approximately one-third higher for subprime loans, largely reflecting the need for more intensive staffing. The typical servicing employee can handle approximately half as many subprime loans as prime mortgages.

Mortgage Delinquencies and Defaults

Most home equity borrowers, like other mortgagors, are current on their mortgage at any given time. Approximately 94 percent are current, compared to 97 percent of prime mortgagors and 92 percent of mortgagors with government-guaranteed loans. Delinquency rates are thus higher for home equity loans than for prime mortgages, but somewhat lower than for government-guaranteed loans.

Default and foreclosure rates differ between prime and subprime lenders in much the same way as delinquencies. At a given time, fewer than 1 percent of all prime loans, fewer than 2 percent of all government-guaranteed loans, and approximately 3 percent of subprime loans are in foreclosure, according to data provided by MIC. Over the life of the loans, cumulative default rates are higher for home equity loans. Cumulative defaults run approximately 12 percent over the first six years for home equity loans, compared with 8 percent for FHA mortgages.

Mortgage terms and loan experience in the subprime market exemplify two facets of the same phenomenon of risk. Home equity lenders take greater risks than conventional prime lenders. They incur higher delinquencies and higher defaults. Because of the delinquencies, they incur higher servicing costs. For these reasons, they charge higher interest rates. They also attempt to manage risk in other ways, for example by offering lower LTV mortgages to protect themselves against the risk of loss.

Within the subprime market, the same pattern prevails. Delinquency and default rates rise with risk. They are systematically higher for subprime A or A-mortgages than for prime mortgages, higher for B than for A, higher for C than for B, and higher for D than for C. The greater the risk, as estimated by the lender when originating the loan, the greater the delinquency rate and the higher the foreclosure rate. What firms expect to happen does in fact happen.

Loans that are thought to be more risky when they are made, do turn out to be more risky.

Real Estate Owned

After home equity lenders take title to properties with defaulted loans, they attempt to sell the houses to recoup part of their losses on the loans. Data from HELLO members indicate that the holding period is approximately eight months, on average, longer than the average for defaulted FHA-insured properties to which HUD has taken title after paying a mortgage insurance claim.

Lenders incur substantial costs on their real estate owned (REO): the legal costs of foreclosure; continuing payment of interest on the mortgage-backed security even though the lender is no longer earning interest on the loan; maintenance; repairs; property taxes; and brokerage costs when the property is sold. On average, these costs add up to approximately 35 percent of the outstanding balance on the loan, and approximately 25 percent of the value of the house itself.

Home equity lenders incur losses on more than 93 percent of their REO. At the other end of the distribution, they get little or nothing back on some 30 percent of the properties. On average, they lose approximately 49 cents for each dollar of their investment in the property. By comparison, FHA loses approximately 34 cents per dollar on its insurance claims.

Thus it is clear that large subprime lenders do not make profits on their REO. Rather, the opposite is the case. Defaults are expensive for home equity

lenders. They lose approximately half of their investment in the property, including both the loan and the
costs of foreclosing and selling. In respect to both
holding period and loss, their experience is worse
than FHA's. It takes them longer to sell a property,
and they lose more money.

CHAPTER 1

INTRODUCTION

Home equity lending is a rapidly growing and changing sector of the home mortgage market that is not very well known or understood outside the industry itself. As defined in this study, home equity lending is the process of refinancing mortgages for homeowners whose credit rating is not good enough to meet the normal underwriting standards of prime lenders. It is important to note that there are two dimensions to this definition: the nature of the loan, and the credit standing of the borrower. Home equity loans are first liens on homes already owned by their occupants, replacing outstanding mortgages; they are not purchase money mortgages, second mortgages, or home equity lines of credit, although the term "home equity lending" has sometimes been applied to the latter two instruments. The borrowers are individuals with some history of credit problems, such as mortgage delinquencies, late payments on auto loans or credit cards, or more serious problems.

The home equity lending industry is so new that there

are no standard measures of its size. It appears to exceed $100 billion annually, and to account for 5 to 10 percent of total mortgage originations in the U.S.[1] Ten years ago, the industry was perhaps one-half to one-tenth its present size. The range of these numbers indicates the degree of imprecision. There is, however, certainly no question that the industry is growing.

The industry even lacks a standard descriptive terminology; it is variously termed *subprime lending, B&C lending,* and *the nonconforming market,* as well as home equity lending. The first two of these terms emphasize the credit situation of the borrower, ignoring the nature of the loan. "The nonconforming market" is a very broad term that includes other types of mortgages and borrowers with excellent credit who wish to buy expensive homes with large mortgages. "Home equity lending," by contrast, describes the nature of the instrument but omits reference to the borrower's credit situation. Nonetheless, it is a commonly used term and seems more appropriate than the others.[2] "Home equity lending to subprime borrowers" is a more precise term but also a longer one; it will be used in the study at times.

Similarly, the firms active in subprime lending are not readily identified in the public mind. They are best described today as "home equity lenders." They have more often been termed "finance companies" in the past, although finance companies offer a much broader range of credit programs. Indeed, home equity lenders typically do not limit themselves exclusively to home equity loans; some make purchase money mortgages and second mortgages. These, however, are usually very minor fractions of their present business. Some lenders also originate both prime and subprime loans.

This monograph is the first systematic study of the home equity lending industry from a public policy perspective. To my knowledge, there have been no academic studies of the industry. A number of Wall Street firms have analyzed the industry, or individual firms in it, from the standpoint of investors in the mortgage-backed securities (MBS) issued by home equity lenders, or from the perspective of investors in the stock of the firms themselves. (At least twenty such firms are publicly traded corporations.[3]) These reports provide much valuable information about the firms and the industry, and particularly about their MBS, but they devote little attention to several issues that are important in a public policy context. They contain extensive analyses of mortgage prepayment patterns, for example, because prepayments affect the value of MBS, but there is usually little discussion of delinquencies and none about foreclosures.

The industry has attracted very little attention from policymakers until recently; the first major federal legislation intended at least in part to regulate subprime mortgage lending was the Home Owners Equity Protection Act (HOEPA) of 1994, which grew out of hearings in the 103rd Congress. Prior to 1993, there appear to have been no congressional hearings or government reports concerning home equity lending. There has been some media attention, consisting mainly of anecdotes concerning individual firms or borrowers, but again no systematic description of home equity lending.

This study considers the following topics:

The nature and growth of the industry. As a framework for addressing the policy issues, the study begins with a description of home equity lending as a business: what the industry does, and how it does it. The chapter highlights differences between subprime home equity lending and the prime conventional mortgage market. It also includes a discussion of the industry's recent growth and considers possible explanations for that growth. The rapid expansion of home equity lending has had important effects on the nature of the industry.

Subprime borrowers. The families that obtain home equity loans in the subprime market are in somewhat different economic circumstances from prime borrowers. This chapter characterizes subprime home equity borrowers, and in some cases subprime borrowers as a whole, in terms of their demographic and economic attributes, insofar as the limited data permit. These borrowers exhibit both differences from and similarities to prime borrowers and homeowners in general. Public policy often focuses on special groups within the population; therefore, insofar as possible, this chapter discusses the extent to which the home equity lending industry serves these groups.

Loan terms. Interest rates, loan-to-value ratios, and other mortgage terms vary between prime and subprime home equity lenders, and also vary within the subprime market. These differences arise because of differences in risk. This chapter provides information on loan terms, with particular attention to interest rates, as they vary among home equity borrowers with different credit situations.

Risk: delinquencies and defaults. Home equity lenders experience higher delinquency rates and defaults than prime conventional lenders, and the risks vary by credit grade within the subprime home equity market as well. This chapter documents the differences and relates them to interest rates and other mortgage terms.

Real estate owned. Like other mortgage lenders, home equity lenders foreclose and take title to homes when the owners default on their mortgages. This chapter presents data on foreclosures. It also reports the experience of home equity lenders with their real estate owned (REO), including holding periods, costs of holding, and losses upon sale.

Throughout this study, the subprime home equity lending industry is compared and contrasted with "A" mortgage lending. Most analysts and most people in the mortgage industry know the prime lending business, and it is their automatic frame of reference. This is also true of individuals in the home equity lending industry; many have recently come into it from employment with prime lenders, and they instinctively compare their current business with their former one. In addition, the study draws comparisons with the Federal Housing Administration (FHA) home mortgage program where possible, and in many respects these are more meaningful comparisons. Like subprime home equity lenders, FHA serves riskier borrowers than do most conventional lenders. FHA is also well-known to federal policymakers concerned with housing and housing finance, and provides them an additional frame of reference.

Risk is a major theme of the study. Home equity lenders who make loans to subprime borrowers incur different—and greater—risks than prime lenders, and their mortgage terms and business activities vary correspondingly. Individuals with experience in both prime and subprime lending often stress the differences between them, differences that arise directly or indirectly from differences in risk.

The study has been undertaken with support from the Home Equity Lenders Leadership Organization (HELLO), a recently formed association consisting of firms active in home equity lending to subprime borrowers. These firms originate subprime mortgage loans and securitize those loans for sale to investors. Home equity lending is the principal business activity of most members of HELLO, although some make other consumer loans and one is a large prime mortgage lender for whom subprime home equity lending is a minor fraction of its business. Some members operate nationally; others have a strong regional focus. Some have been in the business for as long as half a century; others have entered it only in the last few years.

Information for the study was drawn from many sources. In more or less the order of importance, they are as follows:

1. The member firms were the most important source of information; they provided both public and proprietary information about their activities.[4] Most of the data on member firms came from the six original home equity lender members of HELLO: Aames, Access, Cityscape, Conti, Delta, and United.[5] In addition, one nonmember firm, Advanta, provided data for the study. (For convenience, these firms will be described as "HELLO member firms" in the remainder of the text, even though one is not a member.)

2. Quantitative data on important aspects of the

subprime home equity lending industry as a whole, and comparable information for prime and FHA loans, was provided by the Mortgage Information Corporation (MIC).

3. The reports by Wall Street security and industry analysts, previously mentioned, provided background information on the industry as well as some specific information relevant to various policy issues.

4. The Mortgage Bankers Association of America (MBA) has provided data on mortgage lending as a whole that serves as a basis of comparison for home equity lending.

5. Securities prospectuses sometimes included relevant information on some aspects of individual firm activity.

6. Articles in the trade press, and occasionally in the general media, provided some information on specific issues.

The study is partly about the subprime industry as a whole, and partly about the firms that comprise HELLO. The member firms do business in a variety of ways, and do not all collect the same information. Limiting the study to the member firms would have meant in practice reporting on some topics on the basis of a rather small number of firms. From a public policy standpoint, information about the industry as a whole is more important than information about a subset of the firms in it. For that reason, information about the member firms is compared, where possible, with the less detailed information available for the industry as a whole. These comparisons generally show similar patterns for data from the alternative sources.

Chapter 2

The Nature of Home Equity Lending

Subprime Borrowers and Home Equity Loans

Home equity lending to subprime borrowers is the process of refinancing mortgages for homeowners whose credit rating is not good enough to meet the normal underwriting standards of prime lenders. The dominant institutions in the prime conventional mortgage market are the two government-sponsored enterprises (GSEs) that operate in the secondary mortgage market: the Federal National Mortgage Association (FNMA, or Fannie Mae) and the Federal Home Loan Mortgage Corporation (FHLMC, or Freddie Mac). Loans that meet their credit standards and have a principal balance of less than $214,600 are known as "conforming loans." The conforming loan limit is established annually by the Federal Housing Finance Board in accordance with federal legislation. It effectively excludes only approximately the top 10 percent of the mortgage market.

Mortgages do not necessarily have to be underwritten to the standards of the GSEs. Prime conventional lenders, for example, may make loans that do not meet GSE standards for their own portfolios; approximately half of all mortgages below the conforming limit are retained in lenders' portfolios. But these lenders are depository institutions insured and regulated by federal agencies, and they must meet the standards for safety and soundness established by the regulators. Such institutions are not likely to make or hold many subprime loans.

Subprime mortgages are by definition nonconforming loans, and have not been purchased by the GSEs. Freddie Mac, however, has recently announced plans to operate in the subprime market. It expects to purchase $2.5 billion of subprime mortgages (including both purchase money mortgages and home equity loans) during the next year.[1] This would immediately make it one of the largest lenders in the subprime market.

Mortgage loans may not meet normal agency underwriting standards for any of several reasons. A homebuyer or homeowner may have a history of late payments or bankruptcies. The loan applicant may be seeking to borrow more money than the agency underwriting guidelines allow—the debt-to-income ratio may be above the agency limits, for example. Or perhaps the applicant has recently been laid off or is otherwise unemployed.

A homeowner in one of these categories may nonetheless have substantial equity in the present home. Such homeowners may be willing to borrow against their equity for reasons that seem valid to them: consolidating debts, obtaining cash for a specific purpose, or refinancing the current mortgage to obtain a lower interest rate or lower monthly payment. In recent years, refinancing has apparently been the most common reason for such borrowing: interest rates have descended to unusually low levels on several occasions during the 1990s. Also, subprime borrowers may find it advantageous to refinance when their credit history improves (a point discussed in subsequent chapters). Debt consolidation appears to be the second most common reason. It is less expensive for a homeowner to borrow against home equity than to carry large credit card balances. Borrowing for specific purposes—such as education or home improvement—is much less common. Table 2.1 reports the distribution of reasons for subprime home equity borrowing, as judged by one Wall Street firm.[2]

Table 2.1
Purpose of Subprime Home Equity Borrowing

Reason	Proportion of Borrowers
Refinancing	44%
Debt Consolidation	39%
Other	15%
Purchase Money	2%

Source: Bear Stearns, "Asset-Backed Securities: Special Report"

Home equity lenders make loans to such borrowers either as first mortgages, refinancing the currently outstanding loan or loans, or as second mortgages, on top of the current first lien. Traditionally, second mortgages dominated the market. In recent years, however, first mortgages have become the dominant form of home equity lending.[3] These loans accounted for perhaps 80 percent of the business in 1996, compared to perhaps 50 percent in 1993.[4] A Wall Street report on a nonmember firm indicated that first mortgages comprised slightly less than 50 percent of its business in 1989 and more than 70 percent by 1995.[5] Individual members of HELLO report that between 80 and 98 percent of their loans are first mortgages. As in the prime mortgage market, loans may be either fixed rate mortgages (FRMs) or adjustable rate mortgages (ARMs). ARMs are more recent but have grown in importance. One firm reports that approximately one-third of its originations during the last two years consists of ARMs.

The Lending Process
Home equity loans may be originated through any of three channels. Some home equity lenders maintain networks of retail offices that originate loans through direct contact with potential borrowers. Most firms, including those with retail networks, buy loans on a wholesale basis from mortgage brokers or other originators such as banks or credit unions. Firms also buy loans from correspondents—lenders with a warehouse line of credit who want to close the mortgages in their own name. The line of credit is typically extended by a commercial bank, thrift, or investment bank. The warehousing period extends from the closing of the loan to the sale of the loan in the secondary market. To cover this period, mortgage companies obtain funds from financial institutions.[6] Some brokers also act as correspondents. In 1996, correspondents accounted for an estimated 47 percent of subprime loan originations, brokers for 36 percent, and retail operations 17 percent. This is a very different pattern from that in prime lending, where retail operations accounted for 44 percent, correspondents for 35 percent, and brokers for 22 percent.[7]

Retail loan origination is much less important for subprime home equity lenders; they rely on brokers and correspondents for most of their loans. The loans are then packaged as securities and sold through Wall Street firms. The securities are rated by the major rating agencies, including Standard & Poor's, Moody's, Fitch, and Duff & Phelps. A security may carry credit enhancement in the form of insurance from a firm that specializes in that business, such as Financial Guarantee Insurance Corporation (FGIC), Financial Security Assurance, Inc. (FSA), and MBIA Insurance Corporation (formerly Municipal Bond Investors Assurance Corporation). As with traditional MBS, these securities are divided into senior and one or more subordinate tranches, with the latter bearing the first risk of loss. They may include a tranche consisting of the residual interest retained by the issuer, which is overcollateralized with additional loans. Overcollateralization is another form of credit enhancement, either in addition to or in place of insurance.

The industry is not dominated by one or a few firms, at least not nationally. A trade publication estimates that, during the first half of 1997, the four largest firms originated approximately 18 percent of all subprime mortgages (including purchase money mortgages and home equity loans). The top twenty-five firms originated approximately 53 percent. For the same period in 1996, the four largest firms issued approximately 20 percent, and the largest twenty-five firms approximately 65 percent. Total volume increased from $43 billion to $60 billion.[8] The rapid growth seems to be shared widely among industry firms, including new entrants to the market. In both periods, the largest firm originated approximately $3.4 billion of mortgages. Securities issuance is apparently more concentrated.

For 1996 as a whole, the largest four firms issued approximately 27 percent of all subprime mortgage-backed securities, and the top twenty-five firms issued approximately 84 percent. The largest firm issued securities worth $3.9 billion.[9]

The national data may not give an accurate picture of the extent of competition within each local market. Most firms in the industry concentrate their operations on a regional basis, although they also have at least a few loans from nearly every state.

Underwriting Guidelines: Diversity and "Commoditization"

In sharp contrast to conditions in the prime mortgage market, there are no generally accepted credit standards for subprime home equity lenders. Individual firms have developed their own guidelines. Firms typically take the same factors into consideration: the borrower's credit history, including mortgage delinquencies, other borrowing, and recent bankruptcies; the household's projected debt-to-income ratio (DTI) if the loan is approved; and the combined loan-to-value ratio (CLTV) for the home equity loan and other mortgage debt on the property. But they set different standards for each of these factors for a given credit grade. One firm's B loans, for instance, may look like another firm's C loans. This point can be illustrated by one of the most easily quantified factors, mortgage history, which is measured as the number and duration of delinquencies within the preceding twelve months. For a sample of seven firms, some members of HELLO but others not, the criterion for a B credit grade ranges from two thirty-day delinquencies to four, and some firms allow three thirty-day delinquencies and one sixty-day.

Stated alternatively, a history of two thirty-day delinquencies may correspond to either an A- or a B credit grade, depending on the firm. In addition, individual firms change their underwriting guidelines from time to time; a particular firm's standard for a B credit grade may be a maximum of one, two, or three thirty-day delinquencies, at different dates.

There is general agreement in the industry that standards vary across firms. This consensus is perhaps the only general agreement in the industry about credit standards. Several Wall Street firms have published "typical" credit grade matrices for the subprime industry. All but one of those I have seen set a standard of no more than three thirty-day delinquencies for a B grade. (The exception allows four such delinquencies or one sixty-day delinquency.) But these matrices are themselves only general guidelines. As one industry expert has said, "Underwriting to the matrix is an art, not a science."[10] This expert goes on to add that firms need to employ different underwriters for prime and subprime lending. Prime underwriters looking at both types will turn out to be either be too tough on subprime applications or too lenient on conforming loans. In such an environment, variation in underwriting standards across firms is perhaps to be expected.

Mortgage delinquency is only one of several factors comprising underwriting standards. The same point about varying standards applies to the other factors; for instance, maximum DTI or CLTV ratios for a given credit grade also vary across firms.

The fact that underwriting and servicing are not standardized, routine activities has important implications for the operations and cost structure of the home equity lending industry. Because these important elements are not standardized, home equity lending has not yet been "commoditized," to use a term common among lenders. Subprime home equity loans cannot be treated as essentially similar units of the same commodity, like bushels of wheat or prime agency-quality mortgages. Each mortgage application and each closed loan is an individual situation, and each must be evaluated individually. This implies in turn that the costs of subprime home equity loan origination and servicing are higher than the costs for prime mortgages, and that the interest rate spread between the rate charged to borrowers and the rate paid by securities investors is larger in the subprime home equity loan market. These cost issues will be discussed in more detail in subsequent chapters.

The high cost of origination has generated industry interest in mortgage scoring systems. These systems rate individual loan applications and assign numerical scores. The systems were originally developed for the consumer finance industry and are currently used extensively in the prime mortgage market. They include the Fair, Isaacs & Company (FICO) system, based on credit bureau data, and the MDS system based on bankruptcies.[11] Individual scores are developed by both systems, in partnership with each of the three largest credit data repositories (Equifax, TransUnion, and Experian Information Systems); each repository has its own FICO and MDS score for each household in its data base. Some individual lenders have also developed their own scoring systems.

Subprime industry analysts believe that these systems cannot be applied accurately to subprime loans; the applications fall off the scale, receiving numerical scores below the range for which the systems were developed and are reliable.[12] Efforts are being made to create analogous scoring or evaluation systems for the subprime market, and at least two rating agencies have developed such systems.[13] In addition, Freddie Mac has argued that its Loan Prospector automated underwriting system can analyze subprime loans.[14]

Industry executives sometimes speak as if they expect "commoditization" to occur eventually. That may happen, but it does not appear to be on the immediate horizon. As long as underwriting remains an art and not a science, subprime home equity loans will not be commoditized.

The Growth of Home Equity Lending

By all accounts, home equity lending has been growing rapidly in recent years. Subprime mortgage lending now accounts for more than 10 percent of the total mortgage origination volume, approximately $96 billion in 1996, up almost 50 percent from the 1995 figure of approximately $65 billion.[15] (These numbers include both purchase money mortgages and refinancings.) The subprime lending industry is far larger than it was ten years ago—perhaps twice as large and maybe more than ten times as large. It is continuing to grow in 1997, at an annual rate of approximately 25 percent; the volume for 1997, projected from the first half of the year, will be approximately $120 billion.[16] Estimates of its size vary because definitions of the industry vary. Estimates of its growth also vary, partly because of the varying definitions and partly because the industry has grown so quickly. It was not worth much effort to collect information on subprime home equity lending when the industry was very small; therefore, growth rates must be calculated from a base that was not measured very accurately.

Perhaps the most accurate data cover the issuance of securities backed by pools of subprime home equity loans. Table 2.2 shows the dollar volume and growth in asset-backed securities since 1989. The level is lower than in other estimates of industry size, but the rate of increase is larger. The increase is simply extraordinary. Securities volume increased fourteen-fold in eight years. It doubled between 1989 and 1990, and it doubled again between 1990 and 1991. A decline in 1992 was followed by increases of 16 percent in 1993, 57 percent in 1994, 68 percent in 1995, and 105 percent in 1996.[17] Figure 2.1 dramatically illustrates the growth.

Table 2.2
Growth of the Subprime Home Mortgage Industry:
Asset-Backed Securities

Year	Dollar Volume (dollars in billions)
1988	2.7
1989	2.7
1990	5.6
1991	10.4
1992	6.0
1993	7.0
1994	11.0
1995	18.5
1996	38.0

Sources: 1988-1993, CS First Boston, "Financial Companies and Securitization: A Wake-Up Call," October 25, 1995; 1994-1995, John Lewis, "Wholesale vs. Retail Activity in the Subprime Market," presentation on January 13, 1997; 1996, *Inside B&C Lending*, January 6, 1997

Figure 2.1
Growth of the Subprime Mortgage Industry: Asset-Backed Securities

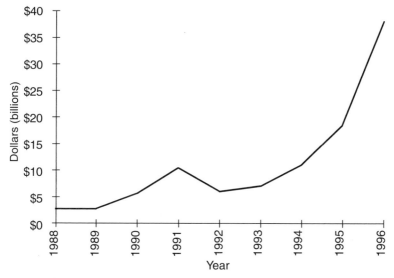

Mortgage Bankers Association (MBA) estimates of nonconforming lending (including subprime lending) are larger and show a slower growth rate. These data include home equity lines of credit (HELOCs) and jumbo mortgages as well as home equity loans and subprime purchase money mortgages. The growth of this broader market is still strong, more than doubling between 1985 and 1991, declining by 20 percent in the aftermath of the recession, and then rising sharply again with an increase of 50 percent from 1993 to 1996. These data are shown in table 2.3. The MBA also reports refinancings as a share of total originations but not as a share of subprime lending. Refinancing activity varies inversely with interest rates, with cyclical peaks in 1986 and 1993. How much of this is subprime refinancing cannot be ascertained from the available data.

Table 2.3
Growth of the Nonconforming Home Mortgage
Industry: Mortgage Originations

Year	Dollar Volume (billions)
1985	48
1986	60
1987	67
1988	81
1989	89
1990	90
1991	100
1992	92
1993	80
1994	86
1995	100
1996*	150

*Estimated as of February 1997

Source: Mortgage Bankers Association of America, "1-4 Family Mortgage Originations," April 30, 1996

Member firms of HELLO report extraordinary increases in originations in recent years. The annual reports for five members show that total originations increased tenfold between 1992 and 1996, doubling in each of the last two years (see table 2.4 and figure 2.2).[18] These data refer to only a subset of the industry, but they consist almost entirely of home equity loans to subprime borrowers.

Table 2.4
Mortgage Originations by HELLO Members

Year	Dollar Volume (millions)
1992	506
1993	843
1994	1,333
1995	2,603
1996	5,175

Source: Annual reports of HELLO member firms

Figure 2.2
Mortgage Originations by HELLO members

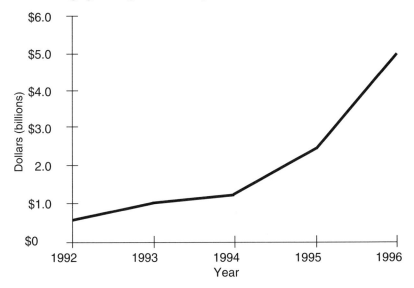

Also, strong albeit non-quantitative evidence of growth can easily be observed:

- There is now a trade publication devoted

exclusively to subprime lending, *Inside B&C Lending*, which published its first issue in 1996.

- The Mortgage Information Corporation (MIC) is developing a subprime mortgage database to complement its established database on prime mortgages.

- MBA held conferences on subprime lending in both 1996 and 1997. At these conferences, firms active in the business explained it to firms that might be interested in entering it in the near future. Other sponsors have held numerous conferences in recent years as well.

- The formation of HELLO indicates a growing awareness that home equity lending is distinct from other types of mortgages and that lenders need an association to represent their special concerns.

Because the industry has grown only very recently, it has attracted little attention from independent academic and government analysts. The Federal Reserve Board's periodic survey of finance companies, for instance, did not separately report household real estate loans until 1996; its previous survey, in 1990, reported only total real estate receivables.[19] Studies of "home equity lending" have traditionally focused exclusively on second mortgages.[20] More recently, HELOCs have been the center of attention.[21] HELOCs are a product of depository institutions, and academic and government analysts typically are more interested in depository institutions than in finance companies and other nondepository financial institutions.

There appears to have been only one recent empirical study of mortgage refinancing, published in 1990 and based on survey data from 1989, before the recent, dramatic growth of the industry.[22] Far more research attention has been given to Reverse Annuity Mortgages for the elderly, which are a much smaller segment of the market.

Why Has It Grown?

The extraordinary growth of subprime home equity lending appears to stem from several changes in public policy and housing finance. In the mid-1980s, depository institutions were the dominant lenders in the market for second mortgages, with approximately two-thirds of the total. The remaining third was reported in the institutional category of "finance companies." Home equity lenders were not measured separately from other nondepository institutions with broad portfolios of consumer credit products.[23]

Subprime Borrowing

Two major pieces of legislation were particularly important in producing the subprime market changes. First, the 1986 Tax Reform Act ended federal income tax deductibility of consumer interest for all purposes except home mortgages.[24] This spurred the development of home equity lending, particularly in the form of HELOCs. Second, the Financial Institutions Reform, Recovery, and Enforcement Act of 1989 (FIRREA) provided the basis for closing many failed savings and loan associations (S&Ls) and established new capital standards for the survivors. After FIRREA, the surviving institutions often found it more profitable to operate as mortgage bankers or to securitize their loans through Fannie Mae and Freddie

Mac than to continue in their traditional role as portfolio mortgage lenders. FIRREA strengthened the dominant position of the GSEs in the mortgage market. This was particularly true for underwriting standards. As portfolio lenders, S&Ls were able to adopt their own underwriting standards (within statutory and regulatory limits). As local institutions, they were also in a position to consider special circumstances for individual loans. They could originate subprime loans and hold them in portfolio. FIRREA, however, significantly decreased their ability to operate in the subprime market, because they had to meet the less flexible GSE standards to sell or securitize their home mortgage loans. This effect was reinforced by financial regulators, who established more stringent examination practices for both S&Ls and commercial banks after FIRREA, in an effort to prevent further financial disasters. Loans to subprime borrowers in a bank's portfolio did not appeal to regulators.

These laws and regulatory practices have created a market opportunity for subprime mortgage lending in the years since 1989. Home equity lenders have moved to take advantage of this opportunity.

Additional impetus has come from the growth of securitization, the process of pooling individual mortgages and selling securities backed by the pool to investors. The first home mortgage securities were issued by the Government National Mortgage Association (GNMA, or Ginnie Mae) in 1971, followed shortly by Freddie Mac in 1972. For many years, the financial markets were prepared to accept only securities with a government guarantee. GNMA mortgage-backed securities were supported by pools of FHA or Veterans Administration (VA) loans, which were insured or guaranteed by the federal government; GNMA added a further government guarantee of timely payment of principal and interest. Freddie Mac and, later, Fannie Mae issued securities that were perceived in the market as carrying at least an implicit federal government guarantee because of those organizations' status as GSEs. Market acceptance of securities backed by conventional mortgages and issued by fully private institutions came slowly, but by the late 1980s conventional MBS were being successfully issued. Further, the financial markets were beginning to accept asset-backed securities based on auto loans, credit cards, and accounts receivable.

In this evolving market, securities backed by pools of subprime home mortgages have been able to earn market acceptance. Investors' willingness to buy them has in turn translated into lower interest rates on the underlying mortgages. At lower rates, more homeowners are willing to borrow.

Home Equity Lending

Demographic and economic factors have tended to increase the amount of home equity for individual households and for the nation as a whole. The postwar baby boom generation began to enter the traditional age brackets for first-time homebuying around 1970. During the 1970s, the unprecedented peacetime inflation encouraged homebuying by anyone who could possibly afford it, including baby boomers. Owning your own home was the best hedge against inflation—indeed, for most people it was the only hedge against inflation. The bond market collapsed and the stock market stagnated, while prices doubled. Not only were there more families in the traditional age brackets for homebuying, but more of them were buying homes. As families rushed to buy homes, they drove prices even higher. By the time inflation was brought under control in the early 1980s, house prices were much higher—in both nominal and real terms—than they had been in 1970. Prices have remained high by historical standards.[25]

The net effect of these changes is that, in approximately ten years, "home equity lending" has shifted away from second mortgages, issued mainly by depository institutions; first to HELOCs, and then to subprime refinancing provided mainly by finance companies, and the volume of home equity lending has grown very rapidly.

CHAPTER 3

SUBPRIME HOME EQUITY BORROWERS

Policymakers have long had a general interest in how effectively the mortgage market serves all groups of potential homebuyers. For this reason, they are interested in the demographic and economic characteristics of borrowers, prime and subprime alike. In the subprime market, there is a further interest in the ability of borrowers to make good judgments about the terms and conditions of loans. This concern underlies HOEPA, for example.

Unfortunately, there are few sources of systematic information about subprime borrowers. Although the demographic and economic attributes of borrowers are important to policymakers, they have not been of particular interest to Wall Street analysts. Nor have individual subprime lenders found it useful to collect and analyze such data about their borrowers for business purposes. Those that originate loans necessarily collect some information to meet the requirements of the Home Mortgage

Disclosure Act (HMDA). Many firms, however, do not originate any loans; they buy them from mortgage brokers or correspondents, as described in chapter 2. Only about one-sixth of all subprime loans are originated through the retail operations of the lenders themselves. Approximately half the members of HELLO do not originate any loans; they have no retail operations. Mortgage brokers collect and report information about the loans they originate, but they are not required to compile it separately for prime and subprime borrowers, nor do they find such information useful.

What does matter to a lender are the credit history of the borrower, the characteristics of the property, and the characteristics of the loan. This information does serve important business purposes, whereas demographic information about the borrower is not directly relevant.

The information about borrowers that has featured in public policy discussions has been anecdotal. This is virtually unavoidable, given the paucity of systematic data. To provide a more meaningful data base, this chapter reports some demographic and economic information from a few HELLO members.

Most subprime borrowers are homeowners refinancing existing mortgages. It therefore seems most useful to compare subprime borrowers to the population of homeowners, to ascertain whom the industry is serving. Data on the universe of credit-impaired homeowners—those who might be in the market for a home equity loan—is simply not available.[1]

The Regional Nature of Home Equity Lending

The usefulness of the available information is limited still further by the tendency of home equity lenders to concentrate their activities within particular geographic regions. Most members of HELLO have (or have had until very recently) a large share of their portfolios consisting of loans on properties within a single state—the state in which their headquarters is located, typically the state in which they began operations. This is clear from published documents such as prospectuses for MBS and for stock. Examples include the following:

- Aames, based in California, has one-third of its loans on California homes, and half on loans in the West.

- Cityscape, based in New York, has well above half its loans on homes in the state.

- Delta, also based in New York, has approximately three-quarters of its loans on homes in New York.

- Southern Pacific, founded in California but now based in Oregon, devotes more than 30 percent of its portfolio to homes in California, more than 10 percent to homes in Oregon, and approximately two-thirds to homes in the West.

- United, based in Louisiana, made more loans in California in 1996 and so far in 1997 than in any other state, with Louisiana a clear second. Loans on homes in the South constitute the largest share of its portfolio.

There are exceptions. For instance, Conti, based in New York, has more loans in Michigan than in any other state, and more in the Midwest than the East.

As the market has grown during the last few years, many of these firms are expanding their operations and becoming more nearly national. For example, some 90 percent of the loans originated or purchased by Cityscape in 1993 were on homes in New York. In 1994, however, this proportion was 67 percent, and in 1995 it was only 37 percent. Likewise, Southern Pacific's concentration in California and Oregon has lessened. In 1993, 40 percent of its new loans were on California homes and 15 percent on Oregon homes; by 1995, those shares were 30 percent and 10 percent, respectively. Conti shifted from having half its loans in the Northeast in 1994 to having half in the Midwest in 1996. Nonetheless, many firms still conduct much if not most of their business in the state or region of their origin.

The regional concentrations of home equity lending are relevant because there are some important regional demographic variations among homeowners, in several dimensions. Most notably, they vary by race and ethnicity.

Table 3.1 shows the proportion of homeowners who are black or Hispanic, divided by Census region. The differences are large. Blacks constitute a much larger share of homeowners in the South than in any other region.[2] Hispanic households are much more common in the West than in the Northeast or Midwest.[3]

Table 3.1 clearly indicates that information on race and ethnicity from a small number of regional home equity lenders will not be a very meaningful guide to the extent of minority lending by the industry as a whole. Important as this issue is to public policy, it cannot be analyzed very usefully for the members of HELLO, and there appears to be no information on this subject for the industry as a whole from Wall Street firms or other sources.

Table 3.1
Minority Homeownership by Region, 1993

Region	Percent of Owners Within Region Who Are	
	Black	**Hispanic***
U.S.	7.8	4.6
Northeast	5.8	1.8
Midwest	5.9	1.2
South	13.0	5.1
West	2.8	10.5

*Hispanic owners may be of any race, including black.

Source: U.S. Bureau of the Census and U.S. Department of Housing and Urban Development, *American Housing Survey for the United States in 1993*

Demographic and Economic Characteristics

For other borrower characteristics, regional variations are less important, although it remains true that information is available for only a few HELLO member firms. This section reports the data for these firms and compares it to the universe of all U.S. homeowners. It is important to remember, however, that not all firms are represented in the data.

With these caveats in mind, table 3.2 and the accompanying charts present summary data on subprime home equity borrowers. The data show that, in most respects, these borrowers are similar to all homeowners.

Table 3.2
Demographic and Economic Attributes of Subprime
**   Home Equity Borrowers**

	Percent of Subprime Borrowers	Percent of all U.S. Homeowners
Household income		
Under $25,000	34	31
$25,000-$50,000	42	33
$50,000-$75,000	16	18
Over $75,000	8	17
Median income	$34,000	$37,000
Age of household head		
Under 35	13	15
35-44	28	23
45-54	28	20
55-64	15	16
Over 65	16	26
Median age	48 years	51 years
Household composition		
Married couple	55	65
Single male*	26	12
Single female*	19	23

*Household head; household may include other adults and children

Sources: HELLO member firms, unpublished data; U.S. Bureau of the Census and U.S. Department of Housing and Urban Development, *American Housing Survey for the United States in 1993*

    The median income of subprime home equity borrowers is similar to the median income of all homeowners and in fact is the same—$34,000—as the median income of all U.S. households. This is so even though high-income households are underrepresented among subprime home equity borrowers, as would be expected. Because there are few high-income subprime home equity borrowers, the distribution of incomes among these borrowers is somewhat lower than the distribution for all owners. [4] Nonetheless, home equity borrowers are not concentrated among low-income homeowners.

Perhaps surprisingly, subprime home equity borrowers tend to be slightly younger than all homeowners. It takes time to build up enough equity to borrow against, and young homebuyers typically make low down payments; therefore, one might reasonably expect home equity borrowers to be older, on average, than other owners. The explanation is that elderly homeowners are substantially underrepresented among home equity borrowers, and as a result the median age of borrowers is lower than the median age of all homeowners.[5]

The most noticeable difference between the two categories is that single men are twice as heavily represented among subprime home equity borrowers as among all homeowners. This category includes several rather disparate types of household: a divorced, widowed, or separated man and his children; an unmarried couple, with or without children, who consider the man to be the head of the household; two or more related or unrelated men living together; and a man living by himself (most commonly either a young man or an elderly one).

It would be interesting to compare subprime home equity borrowers with homeowners who refinance through FHA, but published FHA data are not in a form consistent with the data from subprime lenders. In particular, FHA income data are usually reported relative to the median income within a particular market, whereas subprime lenders report income simply in dollars. Thus, for example, FHA data are reported in categories such as "80 percent of median income or below," "81-100 percent of median," etc. Market areas are defined by FHA as counties or metropolitan areas. It would therefore be very difficult to convert lender data to these categories. In addition, FHA apparently lacks income data for more than 80 percent of its refinancings.[6] Income data on GSE borrowers are also reported in terms of local area medians, and are therefore not readily comparable to the data from subprime lenders.[7]

These data suggest that subprime home equity borrowers are basically the same sorts of household as other homeowners. They are not particularly concentrated among the elderly, who are sometimes thought to be most vulnerable to predatory practices in housing-related transactions. Single women, who may also be vulnerable because they have less experience with financial matters, are somewhat underrepresented. Direct data on the education of subprime home equity borrowers are not available, but education tends to be correlated with income, and there is no evidence that subprime borrowers are concentrated among poorer households. Thus there is no particular reason to think that subprime home equity borrowers are less well educated than other homeowners. They would seem to be in a position to be make rational and informed decisions about their own best interests, including whether to refinance their mortgages.

CHAPTER 4

MORTGAGE RATES AND TERMS

The terms for subprime loans, including home equity loans, typically differ from those on agency-quality mortgages. In particular, the interest rates are higher and LTVs tend to be lower. This chapter describes mortgage terms in the home equity loan market, with emphasis on interest rates. The next chapter discusses the costs lenders incur over the life of the loan, and the last chapter discusses firms' experience with real estate acquired through foreclosure. Together, the three chapters provide a comprehensive view of both the returns and costs of home equity lending.

Data on mortgage terms and delinquencies come primarily from MIC and the member firms of HELLO. The MIC data cover more than one million subprime loans (including purchase money and home equity loans) and are compiled on a comparable basis for prime conventional mortgages and government-guaranteed (FHA/VA) loans. The data for HELLO member firms provide more detailed information on home equity loans to subprime borrowers. There is not much overlap: only two members of HELLO are part of the MIC data base.

Figure 4.1
Mortgage Rates by Credit Risk, 1990-1995

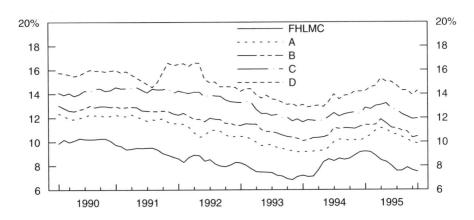

Source: Salomon Brothers, "Home Equity Loan Prepayments: A Study of Equicredit Corporation," April 1996

Where data from both sources are available, both are reported. Generally, the results are highly consistent. Reporting them both permits the reader to make informed judgments about how relevant the detailed HELLO member data may be to the broader market in home equity loans to subprime borrowers.

Mortgage Rates
    Interest rates in the subprime market are higher than the rates on A loans, because subprime lenders have reason to believe that they face higher servicing costs and assume more risk. For the same reason, interest rates vary for different credit grades within the subprime market:

lenders charge higher rates on loans they consider riskier. Subprime rates track the rates on A loans. They tend to move up or down together. Figure 4.1 depicts representative rates for agency-quality loans and for four grades of subprime mortgage, over most of the period of rapid growth in subprime home equity lending. The correlations are not perfect, but the rates clearly move in the same direction most of the time; they are responding to the same market forces.

Wall Street analysts calculate that subprime rates run approximately 200 to 600 basis points above the rates on agency-quality mortgages. Table 4.1 shows a fairly typical distribution of rates by credit grade. The spreads are calculated from data reported by Wall Street firms which have developed subprime data bases.[1] Within each of these grades, particularly the lower ones, many firms have subcategories; for instance, C or C-, C1 or C2 or C3, and so on. There is thus a distribution of rates within each credit grade.

Table 4.1
Mortgage Rate Spreads by Credit Grade

Credit Grade	Spread over Agency Rate (basis points)
Agency (prime)	—-
A-	200
B	300
C	450
D	600

Source: Author's calculations from Bear Stearns, "Asset-Backed Securities: Special Report," and Lehman Brothers, "Home Equity Loans: Lehman Brothers Prepayment and Default Model."

These spreads are not immutable; they vary slightly from time to time, as figure 4.1 indicates, and they are certainly likely to vary in the future. The strong positive relationship between rates and risk, however, is unlikely to change. Subprime rates are below the interest rates charged on consumer credit cards—even the highest rates, those on D grade mortgages, are lower. This difference reflects the higher costs of servicing credit card accounts, and the fact that credit card debt has no collateral. Thus, homeowners who face high debt burdens or unexpected costs may well find it in their best economic interest to refinance their mortgage than to borrow directly or indirectly against credit cards. The monthly interest payment on the mortgage will be less than the monthly interest payment on the outstanding credit card balance.

Data from MIC show that the typical subprime loan carries an interest rate of approximately 10.85 percent, compared to approximately 7.64 percent for prime mortgages (including FHA and VA loans as well as conventional mortgages in this case).[2] The mean rates are slightly higher, with a slightly narrower spread: approximately 11.04 percent for subprime loans, 8.04 percent for prime mortgages. These rates are shown in table 4.2. They are calculated for loans in the MIC data base as of September 30, 1996. The rates are not adjusted for the credit grade mixture of the subprime loans, or for the year of origination, and thus do not reflect the spreads that have actually prevailed in the market at any particular time. Taken simply at face value, they suggest that the typical subprime loan in the MIC data base is of B credit grade, because the spread between the conventional prime and the subprime loans averages approximately 300 basis points.

Table 4.2
Mortgage Rates by Loan Type

Type of Loan	Mortgage Interest Rate	
	Median	Mean
Subprime	10.85	11.04
Prime*	7.64	8.04

*Includes FHA/VA and conventional mortgages.

Source: Mortgage Information Corporation, unpublished data

Firm data by credit grade shows a pattern similar to the overall industry distribution previously described. The spreads for individual firms may vary from the overall industry spreads, but rates are indeed higher for loans graded as carrying more risk. Published data on rates and credit grade distributions for individual firms show a strong relationship between the two factors. The greater the proportion of risky loans, the higher the average rate on the firm's total portfolio. This point is documented in table 4.3.[3] The one exception—the higher rate for the Advanta portfolio than for that of Equicredit—may reflect the fact that a higher proportion of Advanta mortgages are second liens and a higher proportion carry high LTVs. Within a given credit grade, loans with higher LTVs carry more risk to the lender, because an unexpected change in the local market could wipe out the homeowner's equity and raise the possibility of default as an option worthy of the homeowner's consideration.

Table 4.3
Mortgage Rates and Credit Quality by Firm

Firm	Average Mortgage Rate (percent per annum)	Credit Grade Distribution (percent of loans)		
		A	B	C
GE	10.54	88	12	0
Conti	11.66	57	29	14
Equicredit	12.30	46	35	19
Advanta	13.39	49	41	10
Alliance	14.04	15	40	45

Source: Bear Stearns, "Asset-Backed Securities: Special Report."

Other Mortgage Terms

LTVs and loan amounts, as well as interest rates, generally differ between subprime and prime mortgages.

LTVs tend to be lower in the subprime market. MIC data indicate that the median LTV in the subprime market is approximately 70 percent. This is a combined loan-to-value ratio (CLTV), including junior liens as well as first mortgages. By contrast, the median LTV is approximately 75 percent for prime conventional mortgages and 97 percent for government-guaranteed loans. Almost one-quarter of conventional prime loans have LTVs above 80 percent. Almost 10 percent have LTVs above 90 percent, compared to less than 0.25 percent of the subprime loans.[4] Table 4.4 summarizes the distributions.

Wall Street analysts report that LTVs vary by credit grade. In general, LTVs up to 90 percent are available for A loans; up to 80 percent for B, up to 75 percent for C, and up to 65 percent for D.[5] The limits are lower for lower-quality loans because the risk of default is greater, and lenders are trying to minimize their loss in the event of default, protecting their position as well as possible.

Table 4.4
Loan-to-Value Ratios

Data	LTV		LTV Distribution (percent of loans)		
	Mean	Median	Under 60%	60 to 80%	Over 80%
Subprime	—	70	23	67	10
Prime	69	75	22	51	24
FHA/VA*	94	97	1	4	95

*LTV data excludes loans with missing values (approximately 37 percent of data base).

Source: Mortgage Information Corporation, unpublished data

Subprime loans tend to have lower principal balances. MIC data show that approximately 75 percent are for less than $100,000, compared to approximately 60 percent of prime conventional loans (see table 4.5). The median principal amount for a prime mortgage is approximately $85,000, compared to approximately $65,000 for a subprime loan.

Subprime loans resemble government-guaranteed loans in this respect. FHA loans are limited to an original principal balance of $160,950, except in Alaska and Hawaii. Subprime loans have no such limit, but jumbo loans (those for amounts above the conforming loan limit for the GSEs) constitute a very small share of the subprime market. The median principal amount for government-guaranteed loans in the

MIC data base is approximately $60,000.

Table 4.5
Loan Amounts (in $1,000s)

	Distribution (percent of loans)			
	Under $50	**$50-$100**	**$100-$203**	**Jumbo**
Subprime	39	37	20	4
Prime	22	39	34	5
FHA/VA	41	43	16	*

*Less than 0.5 percent

Source: Mortgage Information Corporation, unpublished data

Subprime loans also tend to have shorter maturities. The average maturity is approximately twenty years, but the most common maturity is fifteen years. Substantial minor fractions have terms of twenty or thirty years, which makes the average quite a bit higher than the median. Prime mortgages, by comparison, typically have thirty-year terms, and government-guaranteed mortgages nearly always have thirty-year terms. The general decline in mortgage interest rates in the 1990s has permitted refinancing of thirty-year first mortgages to fifteen-year terms without markedly higher monthly payments. This has fueled the refinancing boom of recent years, an expansion that has covered the spectrum of credit quality, including subprime mortgages. The lower rates have thus contributed both directly and indirectly to the growth of subprime lending.

Rates and Terms of HELLO Members
Data for individual firms within HELLO show a generally similar pattern to the MIC data. On average, loans by HELLO firms have somewhat higher interest rates and

smaller original principal balances, while their LTVs are very similar. Table 4.6 presents average data for HELLO members and compares it to average (or median) data for firms in the MIC data base.[6] The average mortgage rate for HELLO loans is approximately sixty basis points higher than the reported rate for MIC. The LTVs are the same to two percentage points. The average original principal balance for HELLO loans is approximately $5,600, or 9 percent, less than the median balance reported by MIC. With the possible exception of the interest rate, the differences do not appear to be important, and the interest rate difference may simply reflect a difference in the mix of loans by credit grade. Overall, it seems appropriate to regard the HELLO members and the MIC database as providing a consistent description.

Table 4.6
Mortgage Terms: HELLO and MIC

Mortgage Term	HELLO	MIC
Interest rate (APR)	11.66*	11.04*
LTV	72%*	72%**
Original principal balance	$59,400*	$65,000**
Term to maturity	20 years*	—
Value of home***	$82,800	$90,300

*Mean
**Median
***Calculated from LTV and original principal balance

Sources: Mortgage Information Corporation, unpublished data; HELLO member firms, unpublished data

The data on LTV and original principal balance may be combined to estimate the value of a borrower's home. The mean value is approximately $83,000 for the MIC loans and $90,000 for HELLO members. These are both close to the median home value of $87,000 for all U.S. homeowners as reported in the American Hous-

Figure 4.2
Interest Rates by Credit Grade (HELLO members)

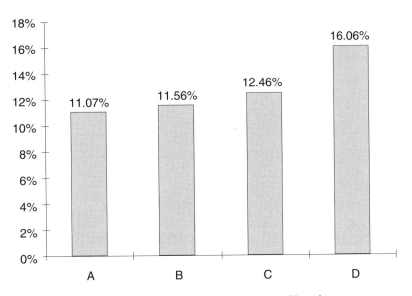

ing Survey. In terms of home values as well as incomes, subprime borrowers are not very different from other homeowners.

Loan Terms by Credit Grade

The HELLO members have also provided information on their portfolios by credit grade. These data are summarized in table 4.7.

Most important is the fact that interest rates rise with risk. The rate differentials are depicted in figure 4.2. The differences are generally smaller than those

Table 4.7
Loan Terms by Credit Grade, HELLO Member Firms

	Credit Grade			
Loan Term	**A**	**B**	**C**	**D***
Interest rate (APR)	11.07	11.56	12.44	16.06
LTV	75%	73%	68%	60%
Original principal balance	$66,200	$58,500	$51,500	$56,700
Term to maturity	259 months	252 months	254 months	276 months
Value of home**	$88,500	$80,400	$75,600	$95,600

*Not all firms have a category of D grade mortgages.
**Calculated from LTV and original principal balance.

Source: HELLO member firms, unpublished data

estimated by Wall Street analysts, as shown in table 4.1. There is an exception; the HELLO members' spread between C and D loans is much higher. These differences probably reflect several factors. Some Wall Street firms are estimating or calculating the differences that exist at a given time, but the HELLO data report the differences that exist on a given portfolio, which has been built up over time. As figure 4.1 indicates, a B mortgage in 1991 and a C mortgage in 1993 are both likely to carry a 12 percent interest rate. The absence of accepted industry standards for credit risk is also relevant: an A mortgage is not the same mortgage for different firms. The credit grades used in table 4.7 are the grades reported by individual firms, with no attempt to standardize across firms. Also, not all HELLO firms report a category of D mortgages.

Other terms also vary by risk. LTVs, for instance, are higher for the higher-quality loans, although the differences are not large. Outstanding principal balances are also higher for better loans, with the exception of the D category. For individual firms, loan amounts on D mortgages tend to be lower than for the higher credit grades. These data imply that the average home value does not vary much by credit grade except for loans in the highest risk category. Values are modestly higher for A loans than for B loans, and for B loans than C loans. Owners of higher-valued homes may be slightly better credit risks.

The term to maturity is almost constant across loan size. The very slight variation shown in the table for HELLO as a whole is similar to the variation within individual firms.

The pattern within HELLO is straightforward and

unsurprising: Interest rates are higher, and LTVs and loan amounts are lower, on riskier loans.

Origination Costs, Fees, and Points

The costs of originating a mortgage are generally higher for subprime loans than for prime loans. One Wall Street analyst estimates that the cost of producing a loan is "in the neighborhood of 4% to 8% of the principal amount."[7] The most recent survey, by KPMG Peat Marwick, indicates that direct and indirect origination costs range from 3 percent to 6 percent, varying by the source; retail lending is most expensive and buying from correspondents is least expensive.[8] Origination costs include salaries, commissions, and other personnel costs, data processing, and related expenses. They also include advertising and other expenses incurred in contacting borrowers, and the cost of unsuccessful leads. For comparison, MBA reports the average loan production expenses as 1.65 percent of the loan balance for MBA-originated loans, including both prime and subprime loans.[9]

These costs are partly recouped through servicing fees. In addition, originators charge an estimated 2 to 6 percent of the loan balance in the form of points—an origination fee paid by the borrower and intended to cover at least part of the costs of originating the loan, as in the conventional market. The compensation to the broker or lender may take the forms of both points and interest. Points can therefore be a matter of negotiation between the borrower and lender, in combination with the interest rate. The higher the interest rate a borrower is willing to pay, the fewer points may be charged, and conversely. The lender also receives income because the interest rate paid by the borrower is higher than the interest rate received by the security investor.

CHAPTER 5

COSTS AND RISKS OF HOME EQUITY LENDING

In managing their loans, home equity lenders undergo a markedly different experience from that of prime conventional lenders. Home equity loans to subprime borrowers are more expensive to service as well as to originate. Subprime loans prepay more rapidly. They have higher delinquency rates, higher default rates, and higher rates of foreclosure. The differences are substantial. All of them arise because home equity loans carry greater risks for lenders than do conventional loans to prime borrowers.

Servicing Costs

Servicing costs appear to run approximately one-third higher for subprime loans. This figure is based on servicing data from Advanta, which besides being a subprime lender also handles servicing for other lenders.[1] Panel A of table 5.1 and figure 5.1 show the difference and disaggregate it by cost component. Annual costs per loan are approximately $170 for B/C loans, on average, compared to $126 for A loans. Most of the difference is accounted for by the higher costs of asset management. This difference reflects the need for more intensive staffing to service the higher-risk loans. As shown in panel B of table 5.1, a typical employee can handle only approximately half as many B/C loans as A ones. The need for a larger staff arises in turn from the higher delinquency, default, and foreclosure rates.

Table 5.1
Servicing Costs by Credit Grade

Panel A: Annual Costs Per Loan

Servicing Cost Component	Credit Grade	
	A	B/C
Asset Management	$ 15	$ 42
Loan Administration	$ 42	$ 47
Indirect Costs	$ 69	$ 81
Total	$126	$170

Panel B: Accounts Per Employee

Servicing Cost Component	Credit Grade	
	A	B/C
Asset Management	3,000	1,500
Loan Administration	1,300	1,000
Indirect Costs	NA	NA
Total	875	500

Source: William P. Garland, "Meeting the Servicing Challenge," presentation on January 14, 1997

Prepayments

As noted earlier, prepayments have attracted substantial attention from Wall Street analysts, unlike demographic characteristics of borrowers, real estate owned, and other aspects of loan experience. This is because prepayments

Figure 5.1
Servicing Costs by Credit Grade

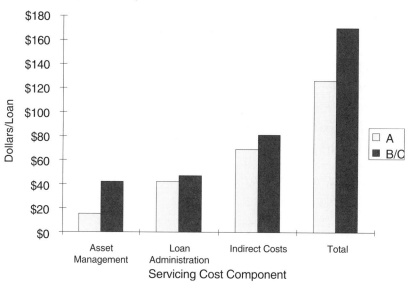

affect the return investors earn on MBS. Several Wall Street firms have developed prepayment models to help them determine how to price MBS, and to help their customers decide which securities to buy.[2]

Prepayments for home equity loans differ from prepayments on prime mortgages in several ways. Prime mortgage prepayments are strongly interest-sensitive: when interest rates fall, homeowners are often quick to take advantage by prepaying their current mortgage and taking out a new one at a lower rate. This has happened on several occasions since the early 1980s, most recently in the early 1990s. Conversely, when interest rates rise, prepayments are less common. A homeowner will prepay a mortgage when selling one home and buying another, but not in many other circumstances. Home equity borrowers are much less responsive to changes in interest rates. More factors influence their decision to refinance, and in practice those factors are often more important than movements in interest rates. High-risk borrowers are motivated by improvements in their credit standing; if they can qualify for a higher credit rating, they can obtain a significantly lower interest rate. They qualify by making timely payments on their mortgages and other debts over the course of a year, and improving their debt-income ratios. Improved money management is, of course, easier to describe than to achieve, but subprime borrowers have a strong incentive to succeed. They can lower their rate by 100 to 150 basis points if they move up one level. A mortgage rate reduction of this magnitude is very large compared to most of the interest rate changes that occur over the course of a year.

Credit rating is more important for riskier borrowers; therefore, interest rate changes are less important. Prime borrowers cannot improve their credit standing, and they are not likely to want to refinance their mortgages if their credit rating deteriorates (although they may have to). Subprime borrowers rated as A or A- are less interest-sensitive than prime borrowers, but more sensitive than B-rated borrowers, and so on through the credit quality spectrum. D-rated borrowers show virtually no interest rate sensitivity.

Loan size is another factor affecting prepayment. Most of the transactions costs of refinancing a mortgage are proportional to the size of the loan, but there is a component that is unrelated to it. Therefore, on small loans, transaction costs comprise a higher share of the loan. Riskier loans tend to be small loans, as noted in chapter 4. Thus, borrowers with riskier loans are somewhat less likely to refinance in response to a given change in interest rates or other factors.

Anecdotal evidence indicates that lenders may encourage borrowers to refinance frequently, taking out large loans each time. This procedure is known as "loan flipping."[3] The benefit to the lender is the repeated payment of loan origination fees. There are also, however, substantial costs to the lender, which are often overlooked. Each new loan involves prepayment of the previous loan. If the loan is securitized in an MBS, the prepayment goes directly to the investor. Thus, from the investor's standpoint, prepayment is undesirable. It shortens the term of the loan and changes the rate of return; in general, it alters the investor's portfolio and returns part of the invested principal before it is expected. If interest rates are falling, the investor will be unable to reinvest the principal at the same rate and will incur a lower rate of return.

For these reasons, Wall Street firms closely analyze prepayment patterns. Subprime mortgages normally prepay more rapidly than prime mortgages, and some prepayments are expected; prepayments are also more rapid on riskier loans, because of the borrower's incentive to reduce his payment by improving his credit rating. These patterns are factored into the pricing of mortgage-backed securities. When an MBS is issued, the loan pool underlying it is predicted to prepay at a specific rate; the investor buys a security with the expectation that borrowers will pay off the underlying mortgages at a rate that can be predicted with reasonable accuracy. Unexpected prepayments change the

value of the security and reduce the value of the investment. Lenders must maintain the loan pool at least at
the size implied by the projection, or suffer financial
penalties either as a direct payment to the investor or
indirectly in the form of lower returns when securitizing
its next package of loans. The securitization process
thus discourages "flipping."

Delinquencies

A key factor in the success of any subprime
lender is its ability to minimize payment delinquency
and to cure delinquency when it occurs. Approximately 94 of every 100 subprime borrowers are current on their mortgage. They either consistently make
timely payments on the loan or have caught up with
any delinquency. For comparison, approximately 97
of every 100 prime conventional borrowers are current. Therefore, delinquency rates are substantially
higher on subprime loans. Delinquencies are less fre-
quent, however, on subprime loans than they are on
government-guaranteed loans: approximately 93 of
every 100 VA borrowers, and 92 of every 100 FHA
borrowers, are current.

Table 5.2 compares delinquencies for conventional prime mortgages, those with government guar-
antees through FHA or VA, and subprime loans. The
data come from three sources. First is the MBA's
quarterly mortgage delinquency survey, which has
long been recognized as the standard source of information on this subject. MBA surveys a large
sample of its members and other lenders. It does not
disaggregate prime and subprime conventional loans.
This disaggregation is available in the MIC data base,

which includes twenty million prime and one million subprime loans. The third source is member
firms of HELLO, including both unpublished data
and data published in recent securities prospectuses.
Among these three sources, there are two sets of
reported delinquency rates for each type of loan. MBA
and MIC both report delinquencies for prime conventional and government-guaranteed mortgages, and
MIC and HELLO both report delinquencies for
subprime loans.[4] The patterns from each data source
are broadly consistent for each loan category.

Table 5.2
Delinquency Rates

	Percent of accounts delinquent			
	30 days	**60 days**	**90+ days**	**Total**
MBA				
Total	2.9	0.7	0.6	4.2
Conventional	2.0	0.4	0.3	2.7
FHA	5.3	1.3	1.3	7.9
VA	4.5	1.1	1.1	6.7
MIC				
FHA/VA	5.3	1.3	1.5	8.1
Prime Conventional	1.8	0.4	0.3	2.5
Subprime	3.7	1.0	1.9	6.6
HELLO	3.8	1.2	1.5	6.5

Sources: Mortgage Bankers Association, "National Delinquency Survey,"
September 1996; Mortgage Information Corporation, unpublished data as
of September 1996; HELLO member firms, unpublished data

As the data in table 5.2 indicate, the overall delinquency rate on subprime mortgages is more than double the rate on prime conventional loans. This is true for either measure of subprime delinquencies compared to either measure for prime loans. There is also an important difference in the length of delinquencies. For conventional mortgages, few borrowers are behind by more than one payment. In the subprime market, many are behind by three or more. At the same time, the subprime delinquency rate is lower than the rate on FHA mortgages. This difference occurs entirely in the thirty day category, however; the ninety day delinquency rate for subprime loans is as high as or higher than the rate for government-guaranteed loans. The comparison is similar for VA loans.

Within the subprime market, delinquencies vary by credit grade, in a clear and simple way: the lower the credit grade, the higher the delinquency rate. The pattern is marked in both the MIC and HELLO member data, as shown in table 5.3. Delinquencies are systematically and consistently higher for A and A- loans than for prime mortgages, higher for B than for A and A-, higher for C than for B, and (reported only for the HELLO members) higher for D than for C.[5]

Figures 5.2 and 5.3 illustrate the relationship between credit grade and delinquency from table 5.3. Figure 5.2 also depicts the differences between prime, subprime, and government-guaranteed mortgages, as reported by MIC in table 5.2.

Figure 5.2
Delinquency Rates by Credit Grade (Mortgage Information Corporation)

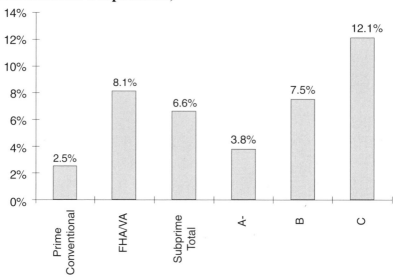

Figure 5.3
Delinquency Rates by Credit Grade (HELLO members)

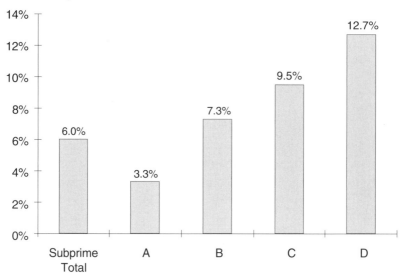

Table 5.3
Delinquency Rates by Credit Grade

Panel A: Mortgage Information Corporation

	Credit Grade Delinquency			
	30 days	60 days	90 days	Total
Subprime Total	3.7	1.0	1.9	6.6
A-	2.3	0.5	1.0	3.8
B	4.2	1.1	2.2	7.5
C	6.3	2.0	3.8	12.1
FHA/VA	5.3	1.3	1.5	8.1
Prime Conventional	1.8	0.4	0.3	2.5

Panel B: HELLO Members

	Credit Grade Delinquency			
	30 days	60 days	90 days	Total
Subprime Total	3.8	1.2	1.0	6.0
A	2.1	0.6	0.6	3.3
B	4.6	1.4	1.3	7.3
C	6.1	1.9	1.5	9.5
D	7.5	2.8	2.4	12.7

Sources: Mortgage Information Corporation, unpublished data; HELLO member firms, unpublished data

Published data for individual firms are consistent with this pattern. Table 5.4, taken from a Wall Street firm's analysis of the subprime home equity loan market, reports delinquencies for five members of HELLO and two other firms as of the first quarter of 1996. Delinquency rates for all but one firm are higher than the rate for prime loans shown in table 5.3. There are also marked differences in delinquencies between firms. The highest rate is more than six times the lowest. These differences in delinquencies appear to reflect differences in the quality of loans. Different firms choose to specialize in different segments of the quality spectrum. Those that concentrate on the lowest quality loans have the highest delinquency rates. This can be seen in table 5.4, which shows average LTV by firm as well as delinquency rate. As discussed in the previous chapter, LTVs are lower for lower-quality loans, as firms seek to protect themselves against losses on loans that are especially likely to default. The highest rate is for a firm described as "the largest publicly traded C/D lender."[6]

Table 5.4
Delinquencies and Risk by Firm

Firm	Delinquency Rate, percent (includes REO)	Average LTV, percent
Conti	2.5	NA
Southern Pacific	3.3	73
RAC	4.2	95-100
The Money Store	4.9	69
Cityscape	5.5	70
United	7.6	70
Aames	15.7	60

Source: Montgomery Securities, "The Subprime Mortgage Finance Industry: Home, Sweet Home," p. 30

Delinquencies translate directly into servicing costs. Advanta, for example, reports that servicing employees find it necessary to make eight to ten calls per delinquent payment, which certainly adds to a firm's costs.

Subprime borrowers seem to take a different view of the mortgage than conventional A credit homeowners. On some loan portfolios, "first payment delinquencies" may run as high as 25 percent. There also appears to be a seasonal pattern to delinquencies. Some borrowers skip their payment in December so that they can buy Christmas presents; they plan to make it up when they receive their income tax refund. In the words of one servicing executive, "This subprime business is not for the faint of heart."[7]

Defaults and Foreclosures

Defaults differ between prime and subprime lenders, and within the subprime market, in much the same way as delinquencies. Defaults and foreclosures are higher for subprime loans, and they vary systematically by credit grade.

Table 5.5 and figures 5.4 and 5.5 report foreclosure rates. Panel A of the table reports overall rates for prime conventional, government-guaranteed, and subprime mortgages, based on MIC data. As of September 1996, fewer than 1 percent of all prime loans, fewer than 2 percent of government-guaranteed loans, and approximately 3 percent of subprime loans were in foreclosure. Figures 5.4 and 5.5 present foreclosures in the same format as figures 5.2 and 5.3 present delinquencies, with the MIC data in the first of each pair of figures and the HELLO data in the second. The parallels are striking. MIC foreclosures are consistently just about half of the total delinquencies; HELLO foreclosures are usually approximately 60 percent of delinquencies.

Figure 5.4
Foreclosure Rates by Credit Grade (Mortgage Information Corporation)

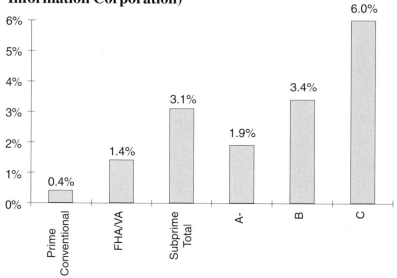

Figure 5.5
Foreclosure Rates by Credit Grade (HELLO members)

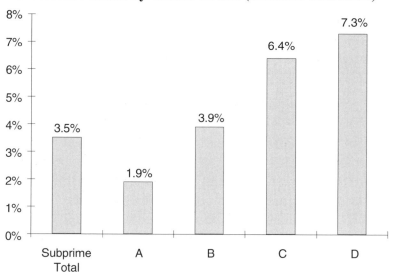

Table 5.5
Foreclosure Rates by Credit Grade

Panel A: Mortgage Information Corporation

Credit Grade	Foreclosures (percent)
Subprime Total	3.1
A-	1.9
B	3.4
C	6.0
FHA/VA	1.4
Prime Conventional	0.4

Panel B: HELLO Members

Credit Grade	Foreclosures (percent)
Subprime Total	3.5
A	1.9
B	3.9
C	6.4
D	7.3

Sources: Mortgage Information Corporation, unpublished data; HELLO member firms, unpublished data

The table and figures also show foreclosure rates by credit quality, as reported by both MIC and HELLO members. The relationship is strong: foreclosures are higher for lower-graded loans. There is a large difference between prime loans and even the highest grade of subprime loan: foreclosures are almost five times as high for A- (or subprime A) loans as for prime conventional loans. Within the subprime category, foreclosures increase as credit quality declines in approximately the same manner as delinquencies. For instance, both delinquencies and fore-closures on C loans are approximately three times as high as on A- loans. Data for HELLO member firms, shown in the lower panel of table 5.5, are generally consistent with the MIC data. HELLO members report somewhat higher foreclosure rates, overall and in most categories.

These data refer to loans in foreclosure at a given point in time. For some purposes it is more useful to measure the cumulative foreclosure rate for loans originated during a given year. This information is not available for subprime loans over any extended period of time: the growth of the subprime market is too recent to permit extensive meaningful comparisons with other loans. Cumulative conditional default rates have been estimated by one Wall Street firm, however, for subprime loans, based on data for four home equity lenders. After six years, approximately 13 percent of mortgages were in default.[8] In addition, information about cumulative default rates has been published by United in its 10-K report to the Securities and Exchange Commission. The United portfolio consists largely of home equity loans to subprime borrowers. The United data indicate that defaults were approximately 11 to 12 percent of the portfolio after six years.

These default rates are higher than the rate for FHA, as reported in actuarial studies of FHA Mutual Mortgage Insurance Fund. After six years, FHA defaults are approximately 8 percent of its insurance portfolio.[9] It is difficult to compare the year-to-year patterns, but they appear to differ in two ways. FHA defaults rise more slowly; in each year they run approximately 1 percent of portfolio lower than subprime rates. Also, the peak default years are later for FHA. Subprime defaults peak in the second year of the mortgage, but FHA defaults peak during the fourth to sixth years.

FHA is probably the most appropriate context for evaluating the temporal pattern of subprime home equity loan foreclosures. FHA has the public purpose of promoting homeownership among households that pose higher credit risks than private lenders are able to bear. Any mortgage foreclosure may attract attention, particularly with respect to the consequences for the homeowner. This is true of subprime and prime borrowers alike. The consequences can be tragic—the loss of a home that may represent all the assets of a family, the necessity of uprooting the family and moving to a less desirable residence. Yet, although it is devastating, foreclosure is not likely to be unexpected when it occurs. The data in tables 5.3 and 5.5 indicate that foreclosure follows as a consequence of delinquency. A small fraction of borrowers miss a payment and their loans become delinquent; a smaller fraction miss two payments; a still smaller fraction miss three or more. Ultimately, many of these long-term delinquent loans are likely to wind up in foreclosure. The process is not sudden: one firm reports that more than half of the loans on which it initiates foreclosure are more than six months delinquent when the default process begins.

Foreclosure has negative consequences for the lender as well as the borrower. It is in a lender's interest to keep foreclosures as low as possible, because the loans are being securitized. Investors do not want to see defaults for the same reason they do not want to see prepayments: in each case the lender receives a repayment of loan principal at a time when he did not expect it and probably did not want it. The consequences to the investor are minimized through overcollateralization, but they can still be undesirable. In addition, from the lender's standpoint too many defaults may increase the price of portfolio insurance, which comes out of the security proceeds and reduces the lender's rate of return. Foreclosures also impose direct costs on the lender. The process of foreclosing and taking legal title is itself costly, as discussed in the next chapter.

These consequences for the lender are not as momentous as the loss of a home is to the borrower, but they are certainly undesirable and give lenders strong incentives to avoid foreclosure wherever possible.

One other point should be made about defaults. Subprime borrowers behave rationally. When home values appreciate, default rates go down for subprime as for prime borrowers. When home values depreciate, default rates go up. The home may no longer be worth as much as the mortgage, and it may be in the borrower's best interest to default, especially if other economic or personal circumstances indicate that it is advisable to move. The pattern is evident in a recent Wall Street analysis of a home equity lender that is not a member of HELLO (see table 5.6).

Table 5.6
House Price Appreciation and Subprime Defaults

Appreciation Rate (percent)	Default Rate (percent)
-20	7.0
-10	6.6
0	2.0
+10	1.5
+20	1.4
+30	1.1
+40	0.8
+50	0.3

Source: Salomon Brothers, "Home Equity Loan Prepayments: A Study of Equicredit Corporation," p. 14.

Mortgage Rates and Credit Risk

Mortgage terms and loan experience in the subprime market are two facets of the same phenomenon: risk. Subprime lenders take more risk than conventional A lenders. They incur more—and longer—delinquencies, and higher default rates as well. The delinquencies generate higher servicing costs.

Figure 5.6
Interest Rates and Delinquencies by Credit Grade

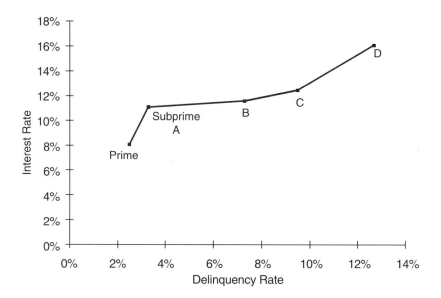

Because these lenders take on higher risks, they charge higher interest rates. They also attempt to manage risk in other ways: they offer lower LTV mortgages to protect themselves against the risk of loss on a default, and they spend more to originate loans.

Within the subprime market, the same pattern

holds. The greater the risk—as estimated by the lender, *ex ante*—the greater the delinquency and default rates, *ex post*. What firms expect to happen, does happen. Loans that are thought to be more risky when they are made, do turn out to be more risky. Lenders' prior assessment of the risk is borne out in actuality; their judgments are confirmed by their experience.

 Tables 5.7 and 5.8 and figures 5.6 and 5.7 illustrate this relationship. The first table and figure

Figure 5.7
Interest Rates and Foreclosures by Credit Grade

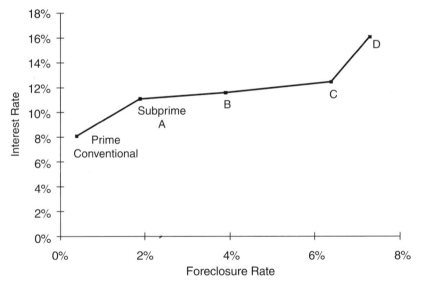

show interest rates and delinquencies by credit grade for prime and subprime loans; the latter pair show the same data for interest rates and defaults. For better-grade loans, rates, delinquencies, and defaults are all lower.

Table 5.7
Interest Rates and Delinquencies by Credit Grade

Credit Grade	Average Interest Rate (percent per annum)	Delinquency Rate (percent of portfolio)
Prime conventional	8.04	2.5
Subprime A	11.07	3.3
B	11.56	7.3
C	12.44	9.5
D	16.06	12.7

Source: MIC and HELLO member firms, unpublished data

Table 5.8
Interest Rates and Foreclosures by Credit Grade

Credit Grade	Average Interest Rate (percent per annum)	Foreclosure Rate (percent of portfolio)
Prime conventional	8.04	0.4
Subprime A	11.07	1.9
B	11.56	3.9
C	12.44	6.4
D	16.06	7.3

Source: MIC and HELLO member firms, unpublished data

CHAPTER 6

REAL ESTATE OWNED

Foreclosed properties typically are acquired by the lender, and they must be disposed of. Firms hold the houses in their own inventories of real property until they are able to sell them. The sales proceeds offset the loss on the defaulted mortgage and associated costs. Sale of REO constitutes the last stage in the life of a mortgage loan for the relatively small number of properties that are foreclosed.

Holding Period Between Default and Sale

It takes time to sell foreclosed properties. Tables 6.1 and 6.2 report the duration of the holding period. Table 6.1 refers to properties that have been sold, and therefore covers the full period during which properties are held in lenders' inventories. There is no pronounced central tendency to the distribution. A few properties are sold quickly; a few remain unsold for more than a year. Approximately two-thirds of the properties are held in inventory for more than three months but less than a year. The typical property is held in inventory for approximately eight months. This is longer than the typical holding period on FHA foreclosures; the average period between claim payment and sale is four months.[1]

Table 6.1
Real Estate Owned: Time in Inventory Before Sale

Time from Default to Sale	Percent Sold
0-3 months	13.0
4-6 months	26.1
7-9 months	22.8
10-12 months	19.6
Over 1 year	18.6

Source: HELLO member firms, unpublished data

Table 6.2
Real Estate Owned: Time in Inventory for Current Portfolio

Time Since Default	Percent Owned
0-3 months	39.9
4-6 months	20.1
7-9 months	16.9
10-12 months	10.6
Over 1 year	12.6

Source: HELLO member firms, unpublished data

Table 6.2 documents the time in inventory for the current portfolio of foreclosed properties, those that have not yet been sold. As would be expected, the distribution is different. Some 40 percent have been in inventory for three months or less; the typical property has been held for five months. At the same time, more than 20 percent have been held for more than nine months, which suggests that the ultimate distribution of holding periods for these properties may be similar to the distribution for those that have recently been sold.

Costs of REO

In evaluating sales experiences with REO, it is important to recognize that the costs incurred by the lender include more than just the outstanding principal balance on the loan. Taking title to a property and disposing of it requires time and money. The costs of REO can be substantial. The costs can conveniently be categorized in terms of when they occur: while the property is in the process of foreclosure, while it is actually owned by the lender, and during the sales process.

Foreclosure

One HELLO member reports the legal costs of foreclosure as approximately $2,500. This comprises approximately 4 to 5 percent of the original principal balance and is approximately the same share of the outstanding principal balance at the time of foreclosure. It is approximately 3 percent of the value of the house.

Additional costs arise because foreclosure takes time, and during that time the lender continues to pay interest on the MBS. The lender therefore incurs interest charges on the outstanding balance without receiving interest payments from the borrower. Several member firms indicate that six months is an average time for the foreclosure process, although the period varies widely by state, depending on state law. During the foreclosure period, the firm's interest cost is approximately 1 percent of the outstanding principal balance per month. Some foreclosures are contested and must be litigated, which adds further to the time and cost.

In some cases, the home equity lender holds a second lien on the property, and may buy out the first mortgage to acquire title and complete a foreclosure. This adds sharply to the firm's costs. Its investment in the property becomes much larger than the original loan amount, and the firm must pay interest on the additional amount until the property is sold.

Holding Costs

While the lender owns the property, it incurs a number of costs. Most importantly, it typically continues to pay interest on the mortgage-backed security, at approximately 1 percent per month, just as it must during the foreclosure process. Alternatively, a lender may repurchase a loan out of the security trust pool and then sell it to a company specializing in workouts. This process is costly, however, because the loan is purchased at its par value but the workout company will not pay more than it can hope to recover. Or the lender can turn the property over to a third party to manage and sell, in the hope that the lender will "receive something back in two to five years," in the words of an official of one HELLO member firm.

Like any other residential property owner, the lender pays property taxes. These average approximately 2 percent per annum of the value of the property, or approximately 3 percent on the outstanding principal balance. In addition, the property must be maintained. This includes cleaning up and repairing homes that were allowed to deteriorate when the owner defaulted on the mortgage, which may cost approximately $1,000 on average. As one Wall Street firm notes, "a homeowner facing foreclosure and the possibility of bankruptcy will most likely not take the best care of the property."[2] Once cleaned, the property must be maintained, including such normal household chores as shoveling snow and mowing the lawn. In addition, the lender must change the locks.

Selling the Property

The sale of any home involves transaction costs such as brokerage fees and closing costs. Real estate brokerage commissions run from 6 to 7 percent of the value of the house, or 9 to 11 percent of the outstanding principal balance. Closing costs probably average another 2 percent of value, or 3 percent of the loan balance. Some properties are "walkaways"—likely to be close to total losses for the lender.

Overall

These various costs add up to approximately 35 percent of the loan balance, or approximately 25 percent of the value of the home, as summarized in table 6.3. The figures are necessarily imprecise. They vary from one property to another, according to the state in which the property is located, the strength of the local housing market, the state and local property tax, the condition of the house at the time of foreclosure, and other factors. In addition, some of the figures are estimates provided by officials of individual HELLO member firms. Firms do not find it necessary to include the various components of the costs associated with REO in their data systems on an individual property basis.

Table 6.3
Costs Associated with Foreclosure and Sale of REO

| Cost Category | As percentage of | |
	Outstanding Principal Balance	House Value
Litigation	4%	3%
Interest	14%	10%
Property Taxes	2%	2%
Maintenance	2%	1%
Brokerage Fee	10%	7%
Closing Costs	3%	2%
TOTAL	35%	25%

Source: HELLO member firms, unpublished data

Independent evidence suggests, however, that the cost estimates are probably reasonable. A Wall Street firm estimates total "foreclosure costs" of 24.5 percent of the value of the property. This figure comprises 11.5 percent for accrued interest, 5 percent for brokerage fees, 3 percent for legal fees, 3 percent for taxes, and 2 percent for other expenses.[3]

REO Sales: Proceeds vs. Costs

For most properties, the proceeds from the sale of the REO do not compensate for the loss the firm incurs on the mortgage loan, including the costs of foreclosure and sale. Table 6.4 and figure 6.1 summarize the relationship between proceeds and costs for HELLO member firms. The data represent the most recent six-month period available from various HELLO member firms as of June 1997.[4]

Figure 6.1
REO Costs and Sales Proceeds

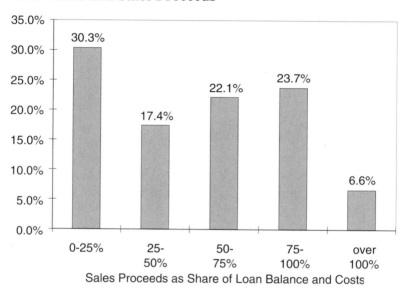

Sales Proceeds as Share of Loan Balance and Costs

Table 6.4
Losses on Real Estate Owned

Sales Proceeds/ Loan Balance and Costs	Portion of Total REO
0-25%	30.3%
26-50%	17.4%
51-75%	22.1%
76-100%	23.7%
Over 100%	6.6%

Source: HELLO member firms, unpublished data

On more than 93 percent of REO, lenders incur losses. On the remaining small fraction of REO—between 6 and

7 percent—lenders are able to cover their costs. On average, lenders lose approximately 47 cents on the dollar of their investment in such property. This includes both the loan balance and the costs associated with REO.

This is a larger loss than FHA incurs on the properties it sells. FHA now loses approximately 34 cents per dollar.[5]

REO Experience

It is clear that large subprime lenders do not make profits on their REO. On a large majority of properties, they do not come close to covering their costs. Defaults are expensive for home equity lenders. They take six months to a year to sell properties after they foreclose, and they lose almost fifty cents on the dollar in the process. On a small fraction of their REO—less than 10 percent—they are able to "make a profit," clearing more than the outstanding principal balance and the costs they incur before they can sell the property. On a much larger minor fraction—approximately 30 percent—they lose nearly everything they have invested in the property, both the amount they have loaned and the costs incurred in the course of foreclosing and disposing of the property. In respect to both holding period and loss, their experience is worse than FHA's. It takes them longer to sell a property, and they lose more money.

NOTES

Chapter 1

[1]As discussed in the next chapter, "subprime lending" in the aggregate, including purchase money mortgages, second mortgages, and HELOCs as well as home equity loans, amounted to an estimated $96 billion in 1996, up from $65 billion in 1995. This comprised approximately 12 percent of total mortgage originations in 1996 and approximately 10 percent in 1995. For the first half of 1997, volume is estimated at $60 billion.

[2]In the remainder of the study, reference will sometimes be made to "subprime home equity borrowers," etc., where it is important to stress the borrower's credit standing as well as the mortgage instrument.

[3]*Inside B&C Lending,* Vol. 2, No. 1 (January 6, 1997), 2.

[4]Any specific data about a firm identified by name in the study comes from public sources.

[5]The three newer members are Countrywide, Long Beach, and Southern Pacific.

Chapter 2

[1]Kenneth R. Harney, "The Nation's Housing: Freddie Mac Studies ABCs of Risky Buyers," *Washington Post,* June 14, 1997, E-1. Freddie Mac's purchase plans apparently refer to a twelve-month period beginning in the last half of 1997.

[2]By contrast, borrowers take out second mortgages and home equity lines of credit mainly for debt consolidation or home improvements, according to a recent study conducted for the Consumer Bankers Association. See Kenneth Harney, "The Nation's Housing: The Loans That Pay The Bills," *Washington Post,* July 5, 1997, E1.

[3]Even as recently as 1995, however, a Wall Street firm produced a report on "home equity loans" that focused almost exclusively on second mortgages, even though it reported on several firms that specialize in subprime refinancing. See SMR Research Corporation, "Second Mortgage and Home Equity Loans, 1995."

[4]Montgomery Securities, "The Sub-Prime Mortgage Finance Industry: Home, Sweet Home," July 16, 1996, 40.

[5]Salomon Brothers, "Home Equity Loan Prepayments: A Study of Equicredit Corporation," April 1996, 4-5.

[6]Keefe, Bruyette & Woods, Inc., "Home Equity Lending: 'B/C' Ain't so 'E-Z' Anymore . . . But it Ain't So Bad," Specialty Finance Series, Vol. 23, June 17, 1997, 44.

[7]John Lewis, "Wholesale vs. Retail Activity in the Subprime Market," presentation at the Non-Conforming Credit Lending Conference of the Mortgage Bankers Association of America, January 13, 1997. Lewis' data source is *Inside B&C Lending.* He reports subprime shares and total market shares (including both prime and subprime). Subprime is estimated to account for 10 percent of the total. I have calculated the distribution for the prime market from Lewis' data and the prime and subprime market shares.

[8]*Inside B&C Lending,* Vol. 2 No. 16 (August 4, 1997), 2. The share of the largest four firms in an industry is a widely used measure of market concentration in economic studies of industrial organization; it is known as the "Herfindahl Index," after the economist who developed it.

[9]*Inside B&C Lending,* Vol. 2, No. 1 (January 6, 1997), 2.

[10]Rudy Orman, "Originating and Marketing Techniques for B/C

Mortgages through Wholesale & Correspondent Channels," presentation at the Non-Conforming Credit Lending Conference of the Mortgage Bankers Association of America, January 13, 1997.

[11]For an introduction to mortgage credit scoring, see Freddie Mac, "Credit Scores: A Win/Win/Win Approach for Homebuyers, Lenders, and Investors," Publication No. 253, December 1996.

[12]Jennifer E. Schneider, "Non-Conforming Credit Lending," presentation at the Non-Conforming Credit Lending Conference of the Mortgage Bankers Association of America, January 13, 1997.

[13]These are Duff & Phelps, and Fitch. See Schneider, "Non-Conforming Credit Lending," and Fitch Research, "A New Look at Subprime Mortgages," December 16, 1996.

[14]Gregor MacDonald, "Automated Underwriting in Subprime Mortgage Lending," presentation at the Non-Conforming Credit Lending Conference of the Mortgage Bankers Association of America, January 13, 1997.

[15]Dennis Hevesi, "Giving Credit Where Credit Was Denied," *New York Times,* June 8, 1997, 9-1. The article quotes Sheilah O'Connor, then editor of *Inside B&C Lending,* for the 1996 data. A separate estimate of $65 to $70 billion for 1995 is calculated in Montgomery Securities, "The Sub-Prime Mortgage Industry," 13.

[16]*Inside B&C Lending,* Vol. 2, No. 16 (August 4, 1997), 2.

[17]Alternative data sources report smaller numbers for 1994 and 1995, but do not change the strong trend of recent rapid growth.

[18]The five member firms are Aames, Cityscape, Conti, Delta, and United.

[19]James D. August, Michael R. Grupe, Charles Luckett, and Samuel M. Slowinski, "Survey of Finance Companies, 1996," *Federal Reserve Bulletin,* July 1997, 543-556.

[20]See, for example, Glenn B. Canner, Thomas A. Durkin, and Charles A. Luckette, "Recent Development in the Home Equity Loan Market," *Journal of Retail Banking,* Vol. 11, No. 2 (Summer 1989), 35-47; and Glenn B. Canner, Charles A. Luckett, and Thomas A. Durkin, "Home Equity Lending," *Federal Reserve Bulletin,* May 1989, 333-344. The latter explicitly excludes first mortgage refinancings, relegating them to a footnote, and the former makes

no direct mention of them at all.

[21]Because HELOCs are primarily offered by depository institutions, they are outside the scope of this study. Montgomery Securities, "The Sub-Prime Mortgage Industry," 40, estimates that less than 1 percent of subprime loan production in 1995 took the form of HELOCs.

[22]Glenn B. Canner and Charles A. Luckett, "Mortgage Refinancing," *Federal Reserve Bulletin,* Vol. 76 (August 1990), 604-612.

[23]Canner, Durkin, and Luckett, "Recent Developments in the Home Equity Loan Market."

[24]Not all mortgage interest can be deducted. The Tax Reform Act set a limit of $100,000 in deductible mortgage interest.

[25]For a discussion of the housing market in the 1970s and early 1980s, see John C. Weicher, "Disinflation in the Housing Market," in William Fellner, ed., *Essays in Contemporary Economic Problems: Disinflation* (Washington: American Enterprise Institute, 1984), 155-204.

Chapter 3

[1]The Federal Reserve Board has recently conducted a Survey of Consumers, including information on mortgage refinancing, second mortgages, and HELOCs. The Board did not attempt to identify subprime borrowers, however, and it is also likely that the sample sizes for subprime borrowers would be too small for valid analysis. Communication from Jeanne Hogarth, Board of Governors of the Federal Reserve System, Division of Consumer and Community Affairs, Consumer Policies Section, September 3, 1997.

[2]The descriptive terms used in the table and the text are those used in the 1990 Census of Population and Housing.

[3]As table 3.1 notes, individuals of Hispanic origin may be members of any race. The decennial Census of Population cross-classifies individuals and household heads by race and Hispanic origin. Most Hispanic household heads are either "white" (52 percent) or members of "other races" (43 percent). Few are "black," "Asian or Pacific Islander," or "American Indian or Alaska native." The classification usually reported in Census data counts Hispanic individuals both as Hispanics and as members of a racial group. In contrast,

the HMDA classification identifies Hispanics as a group separate from any racial group, and does not count them as "white," "black," etc.

[4]In 1997 a new mortgage instrument has been offered, allowing homeowners to borrow up to 125 percent of their equity. These 125 percent LTV loans are typically marketed to higher-income homeowners. They are not a factor in the portfolios of subprime home equity lenders reported in this study.

[5]More detailed data from some firms (not reported in table 3.2) show that few homeowners in their twenties are home equity borrowers.

[6]Harold L. Bunce et al, *An Analysis of FHA's Single-Family Insurance Program* (Washington: Office of Policy Development and Research, U.S. Department of Housing and Urban Development, October 1995), table 4.17.

[7]For example, Harold L. Bunce and Randall M. Scheesele, "The GSEs' Funding of Affordable Housing," Working Paper HF-001, Office of Policy Development, U.S. Department of Housing and Urban Development, December 1996.

Chapter 4

[1]Bear Stearns, "Asset-Backed Securities: Special Report," February 16, 1996, 7; Lehman Brothers, "Home Equity Loans: Lehman Brothers Prepayment and Default Model," March 1996, 7.

[2]Unpublished data provided by Mortgage Information Corporation.

[3]Bear Stearns, "Asset-Backed Securities," 2.

[4]Unpublished data provided by Mortgage Information Corporation.

[5]Lehman Brothers, "Home Equity Loans," 7; Salomon Brothers, "Home Equity Loan Prepayments," 14.

[6]Comparison of averages (means) to medians is necessary because the MIC data report wide intervals in some instances, which makes it difficult to calculate the mean with precision, and not all participating HELLO member firms provided disaggregated data; therefore, medians and other distributional data for the members as a whole could not be calculated. For those firms that did provide disaggregated data, medians and means were generally quite similar;

therefore, the comparison in the text and table 4.6 may be reasonable.

[7]Keefe, Bruyette & Woods, "Home Equity Lending," 38. Separately, one HELLO member firm reports an average origination cost of 8 percent.

[8]Regina Reed, "Survey: Costs, Productivity of Subprime Loan Channels," *The American Banker,* September 19, 1997, 8.

[9]Mortgage Bankers Association of America, *1995 Cost Study: Income and Cost for Origination and Servicing of 1- to 4-Unit Residential Loans,* Washington, D.C., 1996, ch. 2.

Chapter 5

[1]William P. Garland, "Meeting the Servicing Challenge," presentation at the Non-Conforming Credit Lending Conference of the Mortgage Bankers Association of America, January 14, 1997.

[2]For example, Bear Stearns, "Asset-Backed Securities," Lehman Brothers, "Home Equity Lending," and Salomon Brothers, "Home Equity Loan Prepayments."

[3]For example, Jeff Bailey, "A Man and His Loan: Why Bennie Roberts Refinanced 10 Times," *Wall Street Journal,* April 23, 1997, A1.

[4]The MBA conventional data include both prime and subprime loans, but prime loans appear to predominate.

[5]The data in panel B of table 5.3 are not identical to those in table 2.2 for HELLO members because not all members provided delinquency data by credit grade.

[6]Montgomery Securities, "The Subprime Mortgage Industry," 30.

[7]Garland, "Meeting the Servicing Challenge."

[8]Lehman Brothers, "Home Equity Loans," 18. The data are reported only in a chart; I have estimated the default rates from the chart.

[9]Price Waterhouse, "An Actuarial Review for Fiscal Year 1996 of the Federal Housing Administration's Mutual Mortgage Insurance Fund," Final Report, February 14, 1997.

Chapter 6

[1]Price Waterhouse, "1996 FHA Actuarial Review."

[2]Keefe, Bruyette & Woods, "Home Equity Lending," 25.

[3]Keefe, Bruyette & Woods, "Home Equity Lending," 30. I did not see this study until after constructing the cost estimates reported in the text, so the two estimates are independent except insofar as they may rely on the same sources within the industry.

[4]The earliest six-month period ends on December 31, 1996, the latest on June 30, 1997.

[5]Price Waterhouse, "1996 FHA Actuarial Review."

ABOUT THE AUTHOR

John C. Weicher is a Senior Fellow at the Hudson Institute. Before joining Hudson in 1993, he served for four years as Assistant Secretary for Policy Development and Research at the U.S. Department of Housing and Urban Development. He has also been chief economist for the U.S. Office of Management and Budget and for HUD.

Dr. Weicher has held the F.K. Weyerhaeuser Chair in Public Policy Research at the American Enterprise Institute, and has directed the Housing and Financial Markets Program at the Urban Institute. He has been a professor of economics at The Ohio State University and the University of California at Irvine.

He is a past president of the American Real Estate and Urban Economics Association, and received the Association's George Bloom Award for career achievement in 1993. He has been a member of the Census Advisory Committee on Population Statistics, and the Committee on Urban Policy of the National Academy of Sciences. He has served with three national housing policy commissions.

Dr. Weicher is the author or editor of twelve books on housing, housing finance, and related public policy issues. He holds an A.B. from the University of Michigan and a Ph.D. in economics from the University of Chicago.

.

ABOUT HUDSON INSTITUTE

Hudson Institute is a private, not-for-profit research organization founded in 1961 by the late Herman Kahn. Hudson analyzes and makes recommendations about public policy for business and government executives and for the public at large. It does not advocate an express ideology or political position. However, more than thirty years of work on the most important issues of the day has forged a viewpoint that embodies skepticism about the conventional wisdom, optimism about solving problems, a commitment to free institutions and individual responsibility, an appreciation of the crucial role of technology in achieving progress, and an abiding respect for the importance of values, culture, and religion in human affairs.

Since 1984, Hudson has been headquartered in Indianapolis, Indiana. It also maintains offices in Washington, D.C.; Montreal, Canada; Madison, Wisconsin; Lansing, Michigan; and Brussels, Belgium.

Individual and corporate contributors may support Hudson research through tax-deductible gifts to the institute. For information on Hudson programs and other publications, please contact:

Hudson Institute
P.O. Box 26-919
Indianapolis, Indiana 46226
(317) 545-1000